24 FOOTPATH WALKS
IN
HERTFORDS

G000241885

EDITED BY
BILL FROST

PUBLISHED BY ST ALBANS AND DISTRICT FOOTPATHS SOCIETY
1992

INTRODUCTION

The St Albans and District Footpaths Society was inaugurated in 1967. The book '24 Footpath Walks Around St Albans' was published in 1988 in the Society's 21st year. This book '24 Footpath Walks in Hertfordshire' now follows in the 25th year of this Society's existence.

The walks cover a wide area throughout Hertfordshire, and constitute a varied collection offered by our members who have enjoyed these walks on various occasions. The walks vary in length from 5 to 20km, one walk of only 5km has no stiles, and can be enjoyed by families with small children in push chairs. Some are 'figure of eight', offering two short half day walks, which can be combined and completed in a day.

The accompanying maps show signposts, waymarks, stiles, gates and public houses for refreshment en route. Each map has itemised numbering which corresponds to the numbers in the script, and also includes the total length of the walk in kilometres and miles. Frequent compass directions are given to reinforce the script; using these often prevents one from straying off course, particularly when crossing open fields.

Although the script and maps have been checked, changes can occur quickly, and landmarks do disappear. This Society accepts no responsibility for changes or errors. We wish readers much happy relaxed walking.

Bill Frost
Editor

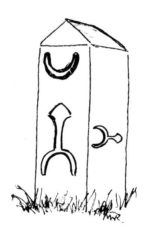

Bridleway sign, West Common, Harpenden

The maps were based upon the 1987 Ordnance Survey Pathfinder maps with the permission of the Controller of Her Majesty's Stationery Office. Crown copyright reserved.

FOREWORD

Our publication 'Twenty Four Footpath Walks Around St Albans' was well received and has been reprinted several times to keep up with demand. We congratulate Emily Frost on her highly successful marketing strategy. Some users have complained that having completed all 24 routes they need more! To satisfy this demand some of us looked for more local walks and those in Harpenden were set down. Then the scope was increased and we looked further afield and drew on the experience of some of our regular walks leaders. The result, in the Society's 25th year, is a further 24 walks within Hertfordshire but in some instances just straying over the borders into neighbouring counties. It has been a daunting task, assisted by many willing members such as Mavis Wynn-Ruffhead who drew the delightful illustrations and others who have made check walks to refine the text and helped in so many other ways. The greatest burden has again been borne by Bill Frost who has walked the paths, drawn the maps and added the important little details which will make all the difference to the reader. May you all enjoy using this further aid to good walking and in doing so you will be helping to uphold the validity of the dwindling footpaths network which this Society, with others, strives to maintain.

Gordon Rowe
Chairman
St Albans & District Footpaths Society

ACKNOWLEDGEMENTS

My thanks go to all the members of our Society who, over some years, have developed these walks throughout the County of Hertfordshire. Others have contributed by checking the scripts and maps, and by suggesting modifications for improvement. Many thanks are also due to Mrs M Wynn Ruffhead for the cover design, and for the sketches of interesting places seen on the walks. Our Chairman, Mr Gordon Rowe has kindly written the Foreword. Our past Chairman, Prof. Ian Morton performed the onerous task of reading and correcting the text and proofs. My personal thanks, last but not least, go to Emily my wife for her patience and help during the writing of this book.

BILL FROST
EDITOR

MAPS

The Ordnance Survey Maps relevant to the walks in this booklet are:
LANDRANGER scale 1:50000
Luton, Hertford and surrounding area no. 166

PATHFINDER scale 1:25000
Luton and Hitchin no. 1072
Stevenage and Buntingford no. 1073
Harpenden no. 1095
Welwyn Garden City and Hertford no. 1096
St Albans and Hemel Hempstead no. 1119
Hatfield and Cheshunt no. 1120

DEFINITIVE scale 1:10000 These show all the Rights of Way in Hertfordshire and are available for inspection at Council Offices or at Central Libraries. Reference to these should be made whenever there is doubt about a route or the status of any particular path.

GRID REFERENCES FOR CAR PARKS

Each of these 24 walks starts from a car park which is located by its Grid Reference. To locate the car park, read the first three numbers of the reference along the top or bottom edges of the Ordnance Survey map, i.e. in an Easterly direction from L to R. So numbers 147 mean that from line 14 go 7 small divisions towards line 15 to get a vertical direction. Then read the last three numbers along the vertical edges, i.e. in a Northerly direction to get a horizontal direction. The intersection of these two directions gives the map location of the car park.

In this example,
G.R. 147 268 locates the Church.
The road junction is at
G.R. 142 263

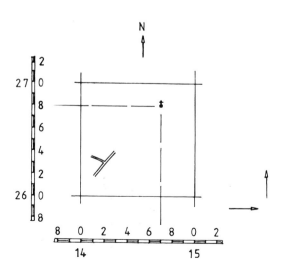

RIGHTS OF WAY ACT 1990

This Act states that:

(a) Paths around the edge of a field must not be ploughed or disturbed.

(b) Paths across a field may be ploughed and cropped, but must be restored within 14 days.

(c) Restoration means making good the surface to make it usable by walkers. Moreover the line of the path must be apparent on the ground so that walkers can see where it goes through crops.

(d) The minimum path width must be 1 metre for a footpath across fields, and 1.5 metres for a footpath around a field edge.

If readers experience any problems concerning paths mentioned in this book, please notify the Footpaths Officer of the relevant Local Authority, and the Secretary of the Ramblers Association (see below). Quote the date, the Walks Booklet reference, and the location given by a six figure Grid Reference or a copy of the O.S. map, to highlight your problem.

Ramblers Association,
1/5 Wandsworth Road
London SW8 2XX
Tel: 071 582 6878

THE COUNTRY CODE

Enjoy the countryside and respect its life and work.
Guard against all risks of fire.
Fasten all gates. Keep your dogs under close control.
Keep to public paths across farmland.
Use gates and stiles to cross fences, hedges and walls.
Leave livestock, crops and machinery alone.
Take your litter home.
Help to keep all water clean.
Protect wildlife, plants and trees.
Take special care on country roads.
Make no unnecessary noise.

Plough, at Plough P.H. Woodside

LEGEND

═══════	Motorway
═══════	Main road
═══════	Secondary road
= = = = =	Track or Lane
▬▬▬ , ▬▬▭▬	Railway
─■── ──	O.H.P. Overhead power line
— — — — -	Path
═══── -	Fenced path
†	Church
✗	Signpost
∧	Waymark
⊢⊣	Stile
G	Gate
f. b.	Footbridge
P. H.	Public House
♠ ♠ ♠	Woodland trees
L , R	The walkers left or rlght when walking the specified route
N,S,E,W	Compass points
m	Metres
G , R	Grid Reference
C. P.	Car Park

CONTENTS

		Page Number
Introduction		2
Foreword/Acknowledgements		3
Maps/Grid References		4
Rights of Way Act 1990/Country Code		5
Legend		6
Contents		7
Walk 1	Breachwood Green, Cockernhoe, Mangrove Green, Offley	8-9
Walk 2	Whitwell, Kingswalden, Preston, St Pauls Walden	10-11
Walk 3	Whitwell, Chapelfoot, St Pauls Walden	12-13
Walk 4	Whitwell, Easthall, Langley	14-17
Walk 5	Markyate, Slip End, Woodside, Caddington, Kensworth	18-19
Walk 6	Flamstead, Pepsal End, Markyate	20-21
Walk 7	Harpenden, Peters Green, Someries Castle, Lea Valley	22-25
Walk 8	Harpenden, Ansells End, Kimpton, Mackerye End	26-27
Walk 9	Wheathampstead, Whitwell, Ayot St Lawrence	28-31
Walk 10	Old Welwyn, Kimpton, Whitwell, Knebworth Park	32-35
Map of 24 Footpath Walks in Hertfordshire		36-37
Walk 11	Wheathampstead, Kimpton, Ayot St Lawrence, Lamer Park	38-39
Walk 12	Flamstead, Markyate, Cheverells	40-41
Walk 13	Kinsbourne Green, Flamstead, Annables	42-43
Walk 14	Circular Walk around Harpenden	44-47
Walk 15	Circular Walk around Wheathampstead	48-49
Walk 16	Wheathampstead, Ayot St Peter, Brocket Park	50-53
Walk 17	Hertford, Waterford, Stapleford, Bramfield, Broadoak	54-55
Walk 18	Flamstead, Great Gaddesden, Jockey End	56-59
Walk 19	Rothamsted Park, Harpenden Common; short walk for families	60-61
Walk 20	Hammondsend, Rothamsted, Harpenden Common	62-63
Walk 21	Harpenden, The Grove, Amwell	64-65
Walk 22	Sandridge, Wheathampstead	66-67
Walk 23	Sandridge, Oaklands, Jersey Lane	68-69
Walk 24	Chipperfield, Felden, Bourne End, Bovingdon	70-71
Bibliography		72

WALK 1

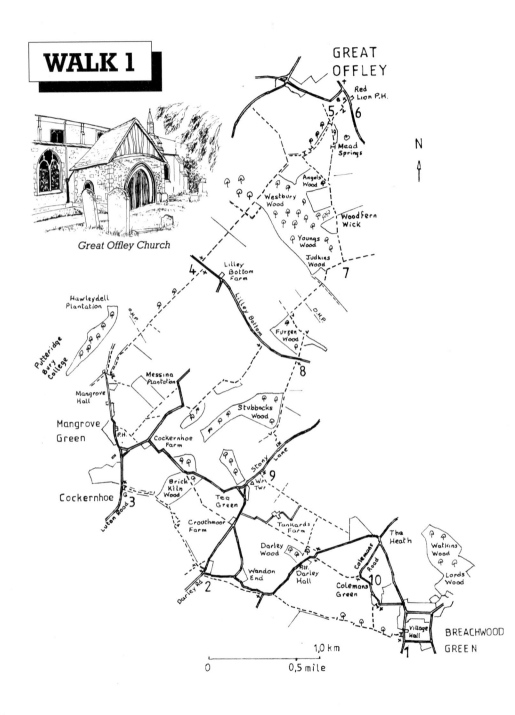

Great Offley Church

GREAT OFFLEY

Red Lion P.H.

Mead Springs

Angels Wood

Westbury Wood

Woodfern Wick

Youngs Wood

Judkins Wood

Lilley Bottom Farm

Hawleydell Plantation

Lilley Bottom

Furzen Wood

Putteridge Bury College

Messina Plantation

Mangrove Hall

Stubbocks Wood

Mangrove Green

P.H.

Cockernhoe Farm

Stony Lane

Wr Twr

Cockernhoe

Brick Kiln Wood

Tea Green

Luton Road

Crouthmoor Farm

Tankards Farm

The Heath

Watkins Wood

Darley Wood

Wandon End

Rtt. Darley Hall

Colemans Road

Lords Wood

Darley Rd

Colemans Green

Village Hall

BREACHWOOD GREEN

N

1,0 km

0   0,5 mile

Total distance 14km (8.7 miles)

Crown copyright reserved

8

BREACHWOOD GREEN, COCKERNHOE, MANGROVE GREEN, OFFLEY.

Park in public car park at the Village Hall, Breachwood Green G.R. 151 219

1 From the car park, turn L (S) along the road and in a few metres cross the road to the signposted stile opposite. Take this path (W) past a large tree L, and follow through some short zig zags. Continue (W) bearing L into a grassy path under power lines between fields. After a further R turn ignore the obvious path ahead and turn L to follow the field boundary to emerge eventually at a bend in Darley Road near Wandon End. Turn L (W) along this road for 100m to the next road junction L. Here a sign-post indicates a path parallel to Darley Road R, which follows this road (W) to a tee junction with Stony Lane.

2 Turn R (NE) along this lane and in 20m take the track L at Ivy Cottages marked Cockernhoe Green. This runs NW with hedge R. Soon a diversion around a small tree plantation is waymarked, but then continue (NW). At the boundary of Brick Kiln Wood the path bears L (NW). At the far side is another small tree plantation with waymarked diversion. Continue (W) between fence and hedge out to Luton Road at Cockernhoe.

3 Turn R (N) along this road to Mangrove Green. Go through the village (N). Ignore a path R, continue on a gravel track past the King William P.H. Go forward over a stile to the brick wall boundary of Putteridge Bury College. Cross the stile in the iron gate, turn sharp R (SE) away from this wall and in 30m cross another iron gate. Here turn L (NE) along a gravel track with hedge L. This clear path marked by some trees continues (NE) for 1.3km to a signpost in Lilley Bottom Road.

4 Cross the road, turn L and in 40m turn R (NW) at a signpost to a path across fields. Go down hill, then up towards Westbury Wood. Continue (NW) along the wood boundary R.On leaving the wood the path soon turns N with hedge R. In 50m at a path junction, turn R (E) with hedge L. In a further 80m where the path turns R, bear L (NE) over a stile, follow a hedge L over a meadow. Cross another stile in the lower corner.

5 Do not go ahead, but turn R (NE) with hedge R. Follow the concrete track through a short L and R out to the road at Offley opposite the Red Lion P.H. where refreshments are available.

6 Return along this same track (SW) to the stile mentioned in para. 5. Cross and bear L (SE) alongside a small plantation L called Mead Springs. Cross another stile into a field (S) towards a corner of Angels Wood. Continue (S) across a field to the boundary of another wood at Woodfern Wick, then alongside the edge of Youngs Wood R to a crossing track at Judkins Wood.

7 Here turn R (SW) alongside the wood edge for 200m. At the next corner of the wood bear L (S). In about 100m go through the hedge gap and continue (SW) downhill. In a further 400m reach the corner of Furzen Wood. Turn L (SE) around the wood and follow the path into the wood edge. In 200m look for a waymark at low level R. Here bear R (S) through the wood and zig zag through trees to emerge and follow the wood boundary R. Continue (S) down to Lilley Bottom Road.

8 Cross the road to a clear path opposite which goes uphill (S) alongside the boundary of Stubbocks Wood R. Here are good views of the surrounding countryside. At the field corner where the path bears L turn R into the wood then immediately L along the edge of the wood R. The path soon zig zags downhill (S) then (SE) to a signpost in Stony Lane. Turn R along this lane (SW) towards the water-tower at Tea Green. In 300m just before the first cottage L, turn L (SE) at a signpost.

9 Look for a path between fields with oak trees 20m on R. This continues (SE) past the end of an access track from Tankards Farm. Ignore this track, continue for 200m (SE) to a path junction where turn R (SW) towards Darley Wood. At the wood boundary, turn L (SE) alongside the wood R and out to Darley Road at a signpost. Turn R towards Darley Hall, and in 20m where the road bends R, turn L on a signposted path (SE). This emerges on to a road at Brownings Cottage.

10 Turn R (SE) along Brownings Lane for 300m. Where this lane turns L, bear R over a stile. Keep L (S) and in 200m meet the tree lined outward path in para 1. Turn L (E) along a short L and R out to the road and so to the car park in Breachwood Green.

WALK 2

Ley Green

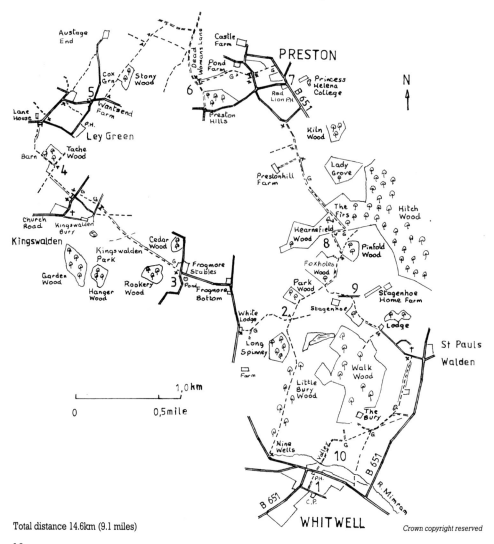

Total distance 14.6km (9.1 miles)

Crown copyright reserved

WHITWELL, KINGSWALDEN, PRESTON, ST PAULS WALDEN.

Park in Recreation Ground car park in Bradway, Whitwell. G.R. 183 210

1 From the car park, turn L and immediately R (N) down Oldfield Rise. Continue along the housing path into Buttons Lane, out to the High Street by the Eagle and Child P.H. Turn L (W) along the road towards Kingswalden passing the watercress beds and river Mimram R. At the end of the beds turn R (N) into a signposted track. Continue for 1.25 km over the hill down to a transverse track with Long Spinney L.

2 Here turn L (W) on a wide track which bends (SW). Ignore the farm entrance L, turn R (W) along a grass path towards the white house out to a road. Turn R (N) along this road, and in 400m at Frogmore Bottom, turn L (W) to a tee junction with a pond L at Frogmore Stables R.

3 At the lodge and signpost opposite, go through a gate into Kingswalden Park. Continue (NW) along-side a fence R, cross a farm track to a stile at a driveway. Cross and continue (NW) across a field passing Kingswalden Bury L to Church Road. Here turn L (SW) and in 40m turn R (NW) at a signpost. Follow this path with hedge L to Tache Wood where turn R along the boundary of the wood.

4 In 70m this meets a farm track at a bend. Turn L along this track (NW), with hedge R, go past a barn R. Bear R (N) around a field edge, follow the hedge R to a stile in a road opposite Lane House in Ley Green.

5 Cross the road, turn R and immediately L at the signpost 'Preston Hitchin' (NE). This road shortly turns R at another similar signpost. Go downhill past Wantsend Farm L and pond R. Continue ahead up the road (E) and in 70m turn L (NE) at a byway sign. This path has bluebells in season. Ignore path junctions L and R. At a tee junction the track bears R (E) to another tee junction with a grassy track known as Dead Womans Lane. Turn R (S) along it and in 500m at a signposted stile turn L (E).

6 Cross the field to a waymarked gate, continue along the track to a barn R where bear R (SE) away from Pond Farm L, then down a slope towards housing. Cross a hidden stile into the lane. Turn L (N) and in 20m turn R (E) at a signpost on a path alongside housing R into Chequers Lane. Turn R (SE) passing Chequers Cottages R to a junction with the main road B651. Continue ahead (SE) to Preston Village Green with the Red Lion P.H. opposite.

7 Continue along this road (SE) with the brick wall of Princess Helena College L. In about 250m oppo-site the main gate, turn R (SW) along Crunnells Green Road. In 200m where this road bends R, turn L (S) at the signpost along a metalled access road. Where this turns R to Prestonhill Farm, continue ahead along the signposted grass path (S). Continue (SE) between a fence L and hedge R into wood-land called The Firs. At the far boundary, turn sharp R (W) to follow the edge of the wood R.

8 In 100m go through the gap in the hedge, turn L (SE) to follow this hedge L towards the cottage. Turn R (SW) just past this cottage. Follow the boundary of Foxholes Wood R, on a path which enters the wood alongside its boundary (SW) for the last 100m. On emerging from the wood, at a field cor-ner R where there is no waymark, turn L (SE) towards the driveway to Stagenhoe. Follow the path parallel to this driveway R (E) then cross it.

9 Continue (SE) round the tennis court R along a track with woods R to an unusual lodge with columns L. This track continues into a road (SE) to St Pauls Walden Church.L. At the signpost opposite the church gate, turn R (S) down a track past the walled garden L on to a driveway road. In 250m where this bends R continue ahead through a kissing gate into a field. Here two paths meet. Take the fork R (W) diagonally across the field to another gate into a gravel track.

10 In 100m this track bends L (S) downhill to cross the river Mimram into housing. This becomes a road called The Valley, and meets Whitwell High Street opposite the Eagle and Child P.H. Continue up Buttons Lane into Oldfield Rise and so back to the car park.

WALK 3

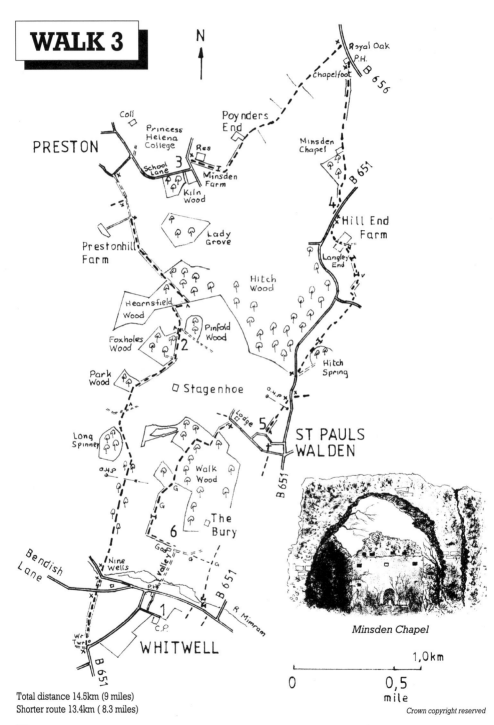

N↑

Royal Oak P.H.

Chapelfoot

B 656

Coll

Princess Helena College

Poynders End

Minsden Chapel

PRESTON

Res

School Lane

3

Minsden Farm

B 651

Kiln Wood

4

Hill End Farm

Lady Grove

Langley End

Prestonhill Farm

Hitch Wood

Hearnsfield Wood

Pinfold Wood

Foxholes Wood

2

Hitch Spring

Park Wood

☐ Stagenhoe

o.H.P

Lodge

5

ST PAULS WALDEN

Long Spinney

o.H.P

Walk Wood

B 651

☐ The Bury

6

Bendish Lane

Nine Wells

Valley

B 651

R. Mimram

Wr Twr

WHITWELL

B 651

Minsden Chapel

1,0km

0   0,5
         mile

Total distance 14.5km (9 miles)
Shorter route 13.4km (8.3 miles)

Crown copyright reserved

12

WHITWELL, CHAPELFOOT, ST PAUL'S WALDEN

WALK 3

Park in the Recreation Ground car park in Bradway, Whitwell G.R. 183 210

1 From the car park, turn L along Bradway to the Kimpton Road B651. Turn L (SW) uphill to the tower. Turn R round the tower into the signposted byway (N) down to Bendish Lane. Cross and continue down to Lilley Bottom Road at the watercress beds. Turn L and in 5m R (N) pass 'Nine Springs' R into a tree lined track. After about 1.25 km, cross a transverse track, continue (N) at a waymark along the edge of Park Wood. Continue (NE) with hedge R and fence L along the edge of Foxholes Wood. On emerging at the corner of the wood, bear L (N) follow the edge of the wood L to a red brick house.

2 Go round the house, turn L (NW) along the access track. In 50m bear R (NW) follow a hedge R to Hearnsfield Wood. Turn R (E) along the boundary of this wood L, and in 150m, turn L (NW) at the waymark into the wood itself. Continue (N) with fence R then between hedges to meet an access road near Prestonhill Farm. Continue (N) along this to the tee junction then turn R (NE) along Crunnells Green. At the junction with School Lane opposite the entrance to Princess Helena College, turn R (SE) along it for 0.5km. Pass Kiln Wood R, to another road junction at Minsden Farm.

3 Turn L (NW) and in 60m turn R (SE) along a fenced path with a reservoir L. Continue (NE) around the edge of a field with hedge R then hedge L to Poynders End Farm. Continue (NE) downhill to the Hitchin Road B656. Turn R (S) to the Royal Oak public house. Just beyond this bear R (S) at the signposted, fenced track uphill. Note the ruins of Minsden Chapel R at the corner of a small wood, continue (S) down to the B651.

4 Do not cross the road here, but bear R parallel with the road along the hedge R. In about 100m cross the road to a signposted path opposite. This goes uphill (S) to meet the access road leading to Langley End. Turn L (SE) go past 'Bridle Ways' L then when this road turns L, continue ahead (S) at the waymark. Continue through stiles with hedge R, then between hedges to the road. Cross the road to a path opposite, cross a field to a stile in a small wood at the top of the hill. Continue (SW) to a track which leads to the B651. Turn L (S) pass the entrance to the Sue Ryder Home R and in about 200m turn R to a path at a signpost. Bear L under the power lines (SW) follow a line of trees to a fenced path between houses to a narrow road.

5 Turn R (NW) along this to a tee junction. Turn R again (NW) for 200m to a colonnaded lodge R. Opposite this turn L (SW) along a path with hedge R. Follow this path as it winds through wood, then along its edge L to a gate into an open field with wood R. Continue downhill with hedge R to a corner where the path turns L (SE) with the hedge R. Turn R at the small red brick Gas Station to a bend in a lane.

6 At this bend in the lane turn L (E) along it and round a bend L. In about 100m go through a swing gate R (E) into an open meadow with hedge R. In 200m this meets a transverse path at another swing gate. Turn R (S) through it and follow a fence R downhill to a stile and bridge over the river Mimram. Cross a small field to another stile (S) into Whitwell High Street. Turn R noting the interesting buildings to Button Lane L alongside the Eagle and Child P.H. Turn L up this lane into Bradway and so L to the car park.

ALTERNATIVELY To shorten the walk slightly, at item 6 by the Gas Station, turn R (S) go down the lane towards the village. This is 'The Valley' which crosses the river and leads to the High Street opposite Button Lane. Go ahead to the car park as above.

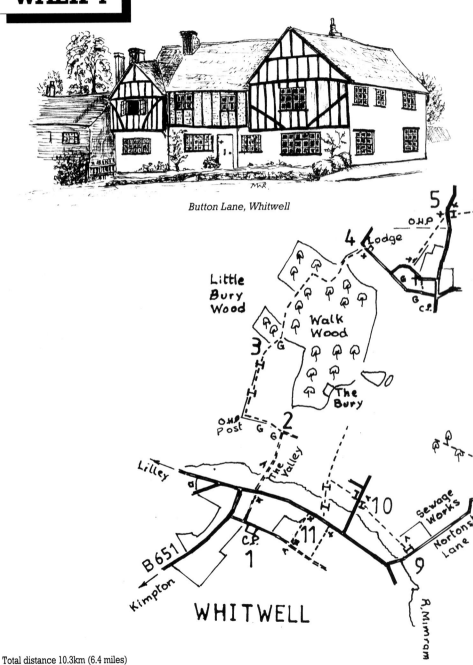

Button Lane, Whitwell

Total distance 10.3km (6.4 miles)

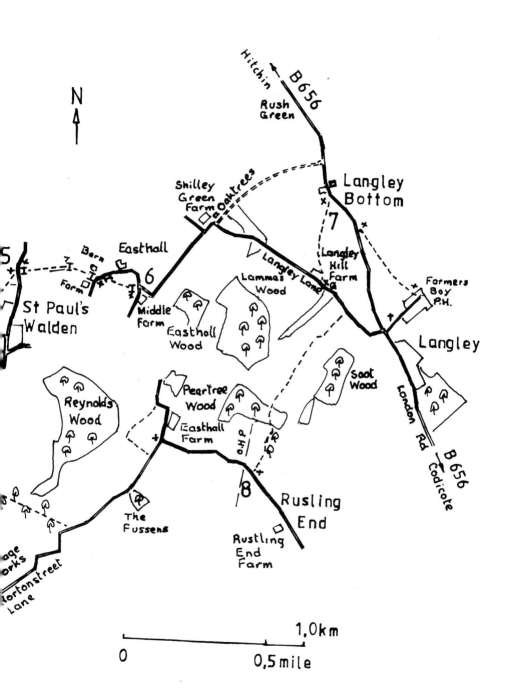

N

Hitchin · B656

Rush Green

Shilley Green Farm · Oaktrees

Langley Bottom

7

Barn · Easthall

Langley Lane

Langley Hill Farm

Farmers Boy P.H.

5

Farm

6

St Paul's Walden

Middle Farm

Lammas Wood

Easthall Wood

Soot Wood

Langley

London Rd

Reynolds Wood

Peartree Wood

Easthall Farm

O.H.P.

B656 Codicote

8

Rusling End

The Fussens

Rustling End Farm

age orks

lortonstreet Lane

1,0 km

0   0,5 mile

Crown copyright reserved

15

WHITWELL, EASTHALL, LANGLEY

Park in the Recreation Ground car park in Bradway, Whitwell G.R. 183 210

1 From the car park turn L and immediately R (N) down Oldfield Rise. Continue along an asphalt path downhill through housing, out to the High Street by the Eagle and Child P.H. on L. Cross the road with care, into the road opposite, called 'The Valley' noting the fine timbered house R. Follow this road (N) over the river Mimram, into a track uphill for 250m to a tee junction.

2 Turn L (W) and immediately in front of the iron gate, turn R into a field. Turn L (W) to follow the hedge L to a power line post at the corner of this field. Turn R (N) following another hedge L, climb along the field edge, go through a swing gate into another field. Note the woodlands of St Pauls Walden Bury R, the birthplace of H.M. Queen Elizabeth the Queen Mother.

3 Continue (N) with hedge then a wood L, cross a stile into a third field, then go through another swing gate into Little Bury Wood. A clear path continues (N) alongside the boundary of this wood L. After a short R and L diversion, the path emerges from the wood, and follows a hedge L (NE) along the edge of a field with views of St Pauls Walden church R, and Stagenhoe House L. At the transverse road note the lodge with Greek style portico.

4 Turn R (E), ignore a turning L, and continue to St Pauls Walden church (where H.M. Queen Mother was christened). Turn L (N) through the church gate opposite the car park. Go past the church L into a minor road where turn L (NW). In 80m turn R (NE) alongside 'Old Meadow' L on a narrow signposted path by a garden fence R. Continue (NE) across a field past a power line junction, to a road at a signpost and hedge gap near a large oak.

5 Cross this road with care, and the stile opposite. Cross the large field (E) past a large oak and water trough R. Continue (E) with hedge R to a stile in the hedge corner. Cross this into another field towards Little Easthall Farm. Cross the stile between the barn L and farmhouse R to a minor road at a signpost. Turn L (NE) and in 60m opposite a cottage with steep gables, turn R over a stile (SE) into a field with hedge R. At the end of this hedge, go past a large opening, bear L to another stile with hedge R. Continue to a signpost at a road junction L.

6 Turn L and immediately R (SE) into a narrow road signposted Langley. Follow this round a sharp bend L, continue (NE) past Shilley Green Farm L. At the sharp bend in the road R continue ahead (NE) on a gravel track past 'Oaktrees' L. Follow downhill past a wood R to its junction with B656 the Hitchin to Welwyn road. Turn R along the grass verge for 250m through Langley Bottom to a signposted bridleway where turn R (S).

7 Follow this bridleway uphill with hedge R into Langleyhill Farm. Go through the farmyard with farmhouse R to a road. Turn L (SE) along this, past a small wood R, and in 200m look for a bridleway R with hedge R (signpost missing at time of writing). This bridleway climbs gently, then continues (SW) downhill across a field to enter a wood as a wide track. Follow this track (S) through the wood to emerge with hedge L into a minor road at a signpost.

8 Turn R along this road (NW) for 600m. At the tee junction by corner cottages R, turn L (SW) into a broad track between hedges known as Nortonstreet Lane. In 700m after a wooded area, L, note a short track R where in a few metres there is a distant view (NW) of St Pauls Walden Bury House at the end of an avenue of limes.

9 Continue (SW) downhill to the sewage works R. At the far boundary fence of which turn R and cross a stile (NW). This permissive path follows the river fence L to avoid marshy areas. Continue to a road near a brick bridge over the river L.

10 Turn R (NE) along this road, and in 20m cross a stile L just before a road junction. The path continues (NW) with hedge and river L to meet a transverse path. Turn L (S) cross a stile and cross the river by a small concrete bridge. Cross the meadow ahead with fence R (S) to a stile by a gate. Go through the yard of Whitwell Mill. Note the disused water wheel R and Mill House R. Turn R along the High Street (NW).

11 In 70m opposite number 22, turn L (SW) at the signpost marked 'Kimpton', go uphill on an asphalt path between housing, with conifer hedge L. On emerging into a field, turn R and follow the field edge R (NW) passing bungalows R. Go between tall shrubs, past tennis courts L into the car park.

Alternatively at item 9 continue (SW) downhill and cross the river to the High Street. Turn R (NW) past cottages with raised gardens L to house number 22, item 11. This enables one to see more of the village.

St Paul's Walden

17

WALK 5

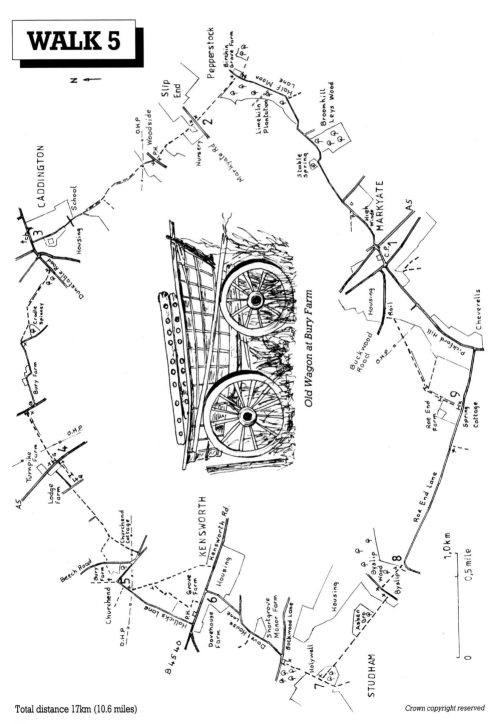

Old Wagon at Bury Farm

Total distance 17km (10.6 miles)

Crown copyright reserved

18

MARKYATE, SLIP END, WOODSIDE, CADDINGTON, KENSWORTH

Park in public car park in Hicks Road Markyate, G.R 063 164

WALK 5

1 Turn L (NE) out of the car park towards the A5, and cross using the footbridge. Walk up Harps Hill passing 'High Winds' R. Where this lane turns R, continue ahead (NE) along Half Moon Lane. In about 2km at the end of the wood L opposite Birchin Grove Farm, turn L (NW) along a path to Markyate Road at Slip End.

2 Cross the road continue along a path (NW) to the Harrow P.H. at Woodside. Cross this road continue along a lane past housing L. Go under power lines, across a field, then along a field edge path with hedge L. Go across a field to the corner of the school fence R into Heathfield Path. Continue (NW) through housing past a school L towards the church to the road junction in Caddington.

3 At the village centre, turn L (SW) along the Dunstable Road for about 200m. Turn R (NW) along a path through bushes, then with hedge L. This turns half L towards Cradle Spinney. Do not enter this but continue (NW) across a field to a sunken lane. Bear L (W) along it through the buildings of Bury Farm. At the road turn R (NW) and in 100m turn L (SW) at the stile. This path with hedge L goes under power lines down to the A5 opposite Lodge Farm.

4 Turn L along A5 and in 50m R (SW) alongside a green boundary fence L by a builders yard. Continue up a field edge with hedge R to a metal gate leading to a lane. Turn R (NW) along this and in 50m turn L up a path with hedge L. This leads over a hill then down to a road along which turn R (NW) to the church at Churchend.

5 Turn L (SW) up Hollicks Lane. In 150m turn L (S) into a field path immediately under power lines. Cross this field (S) down to a large tree. Bear R (SW) at the waymark, and continue down to the bottom of the valley, just to R of two waymarked trees. Turn L in front of them, then R (SW) following the field edge up to houses on the skyline. Turn L (SE) behind the houses for 50m then turn R over a gate into Kensworth Road by a former garage. Turn R (NW) and in 100m is the Farmers Boy P.H. where refreshments may be obtained.

6 From the P.H. turn L (SE) along the road and in 250m turn R into Dovehouse Lane. Pass Shortgrove Manor Farm L go on to its junction with Buckwood Lane. Turn R (W) and in 50m L (SW) over a stile, and up through a woodland path with housing R.

7 After 400m turn L (SE) at the signpost through the woods, then across a field and alongside Ashen Grove L. This passes housing R and emerges on to a road at Byslips. Turn L (NE) and in 100m R (SE) along a path with woods L.

8 On emerging from the wood turn R then L at the waymark, this joins Roe End Lane in 50m. Continue (SE) along this lane for 1.5km to Roe End Farm.

9 At the farm boundary opposite Spring Cottage turn L, (NE) cross the stile signposted to Buckwood Road. Cross two more stiles, continue (NE) under power lines into Buckwood housing. Turn R along the road to the junction where a short R and L leads to the car park.

Kensworth Church

WALK 6

One of a pair of gates
in Half Moon Lane

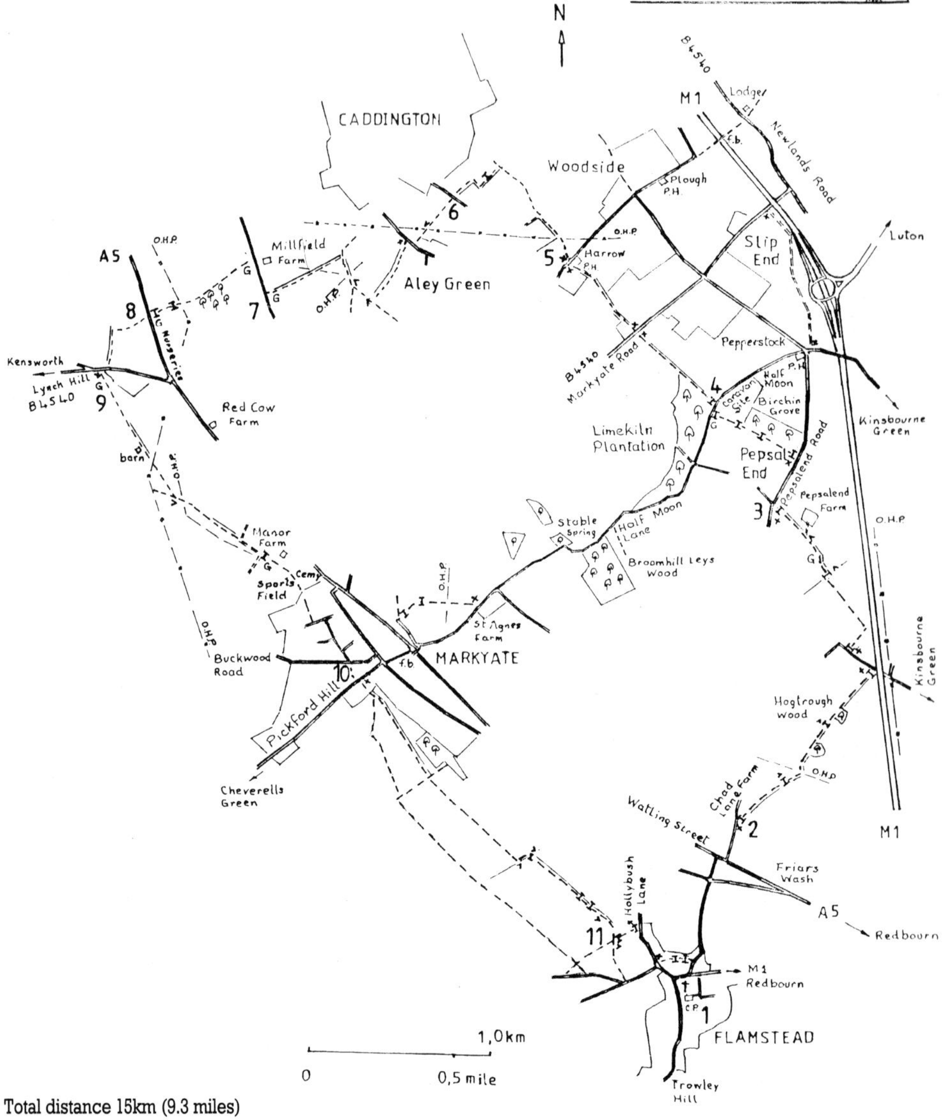

Total distance 15km (9.3 miles)
Shorter route 10.1km (6.3 miles)

Crown copyright reserved

20

FLAMSTEAD, PEPSAL END, MARKYATE

Park in car park in Church Lane, at rear of Village Hall, Flamstead. G.R. 079 145.

WALK 6

1 From the car park, turn L (N) along Church Lane. In 100m at the tee junction, turn L (W) and in 20m turn R (N) down hill to the A5. Cross this with care, go up the hill (N) in 100m turn R (E) along the ancient Watling Street, and in 10m turn L (N) into Chad Lane signposted 'Pepperstock'.

2 Continue along this lane for 300m to a signpost R opposite Chad Lane Farm. Cross the stile (NE) along a path with hedge R, continue down into a valley, then up alongside Hogtrough Wood R into a road by the motorway. Turn L (NW) away from the M1, in 150m at the signpost, turn R (NE) into a field and walk towards the M1 aiming for the yellow telephone box. Just before reaching the M1 fence, turn L (NW) across the field towards a stile in the fence. Cross this and continue (NW) with fence R past Pepsalend Farm R into Pepsal End Road.

3 Turn R (NE) along this road for 300m. At the signpost turn L over a stile, and continue under power lines alongside a wood R. Cross two more stiles, go between fences into Half Moon Lane. Turn R (NE) to Keepers Cottage at Birchin Grove Farm, turn L over a stile immediately opposite the cottages.

4 Continue (NW) alongside a wood boundary L, then with hedge R. Go through the hedge gap and emerge on to Markyate Road. Cross and continue forward (NW) between housing then with hedge R emerge by the Harrow P.H.

5 Cross the road, continue (NW) into the asphalt access track, which soon becomes a gravel track under power lines. Go forward across a field, ignore the path L at the hedge corner. Continue with hedge L to a corner where turn L (SW). In the next corner cross the iron stile, not easily seen, go ahead (SW) into the sports field. Keep to the hedge L, and follow it round a R and L corner. Continue (SW) past the tennis courts R and emerge into a road at a pipe rail gap.

6 Cross the road and continue ahead (SW) across a field under two power lines, then with hedge L emerge into the road in the valley bottom. Turn R (NW) and in 25m turn L (SW) over a plank bridge. Go uphill with hedge R to a transverse path with three way signpost. Turn R (NW) and go forward. At the hedge gap, follow the waymark forward. After crossing under the power lines, turn L (SW) at the next hedge. Follow this R out to Millfield Lane through a gap at a double gate.

7 Turn R (N) go past the Cotswold Business Park and in 200m just before Millfield House, turn L (SW) through a gap by a metal gate. Cross the field (SW) heading for the R end of a line of trees. Continue alongside the wood L to a boundary corner. Bear L across the field towards the tallest tree in the hedge, heading for the A5 road sign. Just under the power line, cross the stile in the hedge by this tree. At the bottom of the next field, cross the stile by a gate onto the A5 by Kensworth Nurseries.

8 Cross this busy road with care, and enter the field opposite. Go uphill for 200m (SW). At the transverse hedge, turn L (S) and follow the hedge R down to a hedge gap by a large chestnut tree. Cross the plank bridge into Lynch Hill B4540. Turn R (W) and in 20m turn L (SE) by a gate into a wide gravel track.

9 Go ahead (SE) past a metal barn R into a field with hedge L, then under power lines. At a waymark by a power post, bear L through this hedge. Cross the field (SE) following the power lines R. This leads to a track with hedge L. Follow this track (SE). Where this track turns R by a power pole, keep forward (SE) over a stile by a metal gate. Go through the next gate into a sports area, follow a hedge L into a road. Turn L (NE) and in 60m turn R (SE) by a seat to a track leading to roads between housing. Cross Buckwood Road to a path alongside Markyate Baptist Church.

10 Continue ahead (SE) through housing, over a grassy area, bear L into Pickford Hill. Cross to a sunken footpath (SE) between houses number 19 and 21 Markyate Park. At the play area take the L fork with hedge L (SE). After 1.25km at a transverse hedge turn L (NE) at the waymark. In 50m just before a hedge corner, turn R (SE) over a waymarked stile. Continue (SE) with the hedge L, cross three stiles to a wooden signpost, then go (S) between fences.

11 In 50m at the next wooden signpost, turn L (NE) cross the stile go over the field into Hollybush Lane. Here turn R (S) and in 150m at a signpost turn L (E) between housing. Cross two more stiles into a lane where turn R up to the centre of Flamstead. At the tee junction turn L and in 10m R into Church Lane and the car park.

Alternatively This walk may be shortened by turning L at item 4 and going down Half Moon Lane to Markyate. The route then being items 1, 2, 3, 4, 10 and 11.

WALK 7

LUTON

B 653

6

Bush Pasture

George Wood

Watbr Cottage

Luton Hoo Park

Someries Castle

Luton Hoo

Lake

Stables

New Mill End

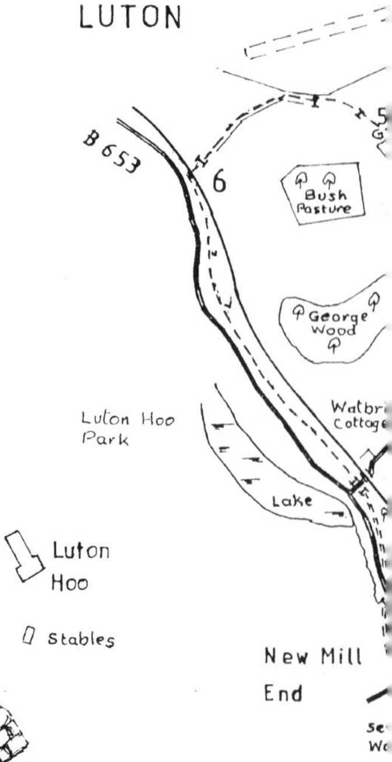

Total distance 16.6km (10.3 miles)
Walk A 11.3km (7.0 miles)
Walk B 10.5km (6.5 miles)

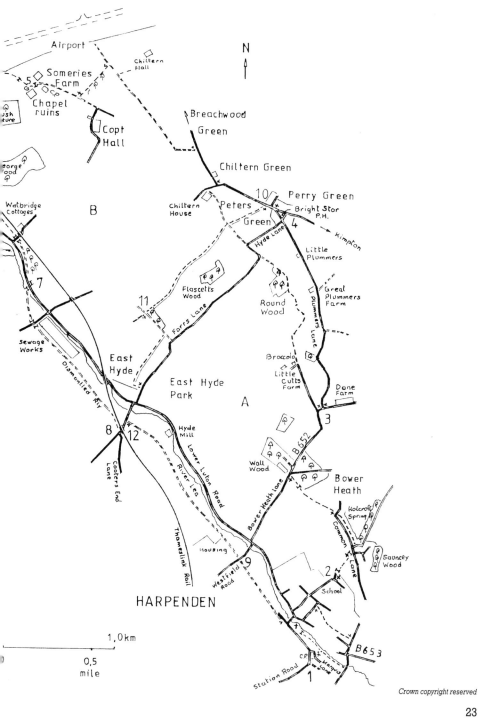

Crown copyright reserved

23

HARPENDEN, PETERS GREEN, SOMERIES CASTLE, LEA VALLEY

Starting from the south, park in public car park at junction of Marquis Lane and Station Road, Harpenden. G.R. 146 150.

1 From the car park, cross Marquis Lane to the footpath opposite (E) into the recreation ground. Follow the hedge L, do not cross the footbridge, but turn R (SE) alongside the stream L. After passing the play area R, note the weir on the river Lea. This may be seen more closely using the stepping stones. On reaching Crabtree Lane, turn L (N) and cross the river by the bridge by the ford. Continue (N) to the B653 main road, and cross it into Common Lane opposite. Go past Batford road L then turn L (NW) into a signed path between housing. Continue ahead with allotments R ignoring crossing paths. At the road junction turn R into South View road, turn L into Roundfield Avenue, then R (NE) into Pickford Hill. Pass the school R, then turn L into Whitings Close. Cross the stile R at the end of this Close.

2 Cross the meadow (NE) keeping to the hedge R, continue through a wooded area and cross the stile into Common Lane where turn L (NW). After a few metres turn R into Sauncey Wood Lane and immediately L (NW) through a gap into Holcroft Spring Wood, which is carpeted with bluebells in May. Keep to a well trodden path (NW) just a few metres from the road (L). At a gap by a bend in the road, cross the road with care, to a signpost and gate opposite. Continue (NW) along a field edge with hedge R. Cross a stile into a small wood and continue (NW) to Bower Heath Lane B652 by a bungalow L. Cross the road at the grassy island, continue (N) along the B652 which soon bends L.

3 At a sharp R bend in the road, turn L (N) along the access road to Little Cutts Farm. Where this turns L, continue ahead (N) along a bridle path passing Broccolo cottage L. This well used path (N) through a wooded strip emerges on to a bend in Farrs Lane. Continue (NW) along this lane for 100m then turn R (NE) along Hyde Lane. At the road junction turn L into Peters Green passing the Bright Star P.H. R.

4 Bear L (NW) along the Kimpton Road which in about 500m bends L (W). Take the next turning R (N) passing the cottages R at Chiltern Green. In about 400m at a circular route waymark turn L (W) into a tree lined bridleway. This meanders through trees and is covered in bluebells in May. After about 1km note Chiltern Hall R, turn L (SW) at a waymark and follow a line of trees between fields. Note Luton Hoo in the distance. At a transverse lane, turn R (W) towards a group of buildings at Someries with buildings in Luton Airport half R. Someries 'Castle ' is worth inspection and suitable as a picnic stop.

5 · Cross the stile passing the 'Castle' L (W), then bear R through a small meadow to a waymarked iron gate. Go through, turn R (NW) with hedge R, cross a stile and continue downhill across a field with airport R. Locate a stile in the corner of the field below a rubble tip and continue forward (W) between fences. Cross a stile by the houses, go under the railway bridge. Turn L (S) at the road B653.

6 In a few metres, climb a stile on L into a narrow field and continue (SE) between the road R and the railway L. Note the swan waymarks indicating the Upper Lea Valley walkway. At the field end cross a road between two stiles (S) into a young tree plantation, follow the waymarks (S) on to the course of the dismantled railway. Continue (S) to steps leading down to a roadside stile.

7 Cross this busy road B653 with care, bear L along it to another stile where turn R up the steps. Follow the zig zag upwards to regain the line of the old railway (S). Cross the bridge over the Lea, pass the sewage works L, and cross a stile into a road noting the former LNER station house opposite. Cross the road bear L, go over a stile (S) and continue with sewage works L. On reaching the iron bridge carrying the main line railway, do not continue under it, but climb the steps R. Walk (SE) alongside the railway L with fields R.

8 At a transverse road turn L under a bridge and in a few metres, at a swan waymark climb the bank R to continue (SE) along the old rail route. Note the Lea and Hyde Mill L. Follow this clear path (SE) with fence L for about 1.5km, then go up the steps to Westfield Road.

9 Cross the road and continue (SE) along the path opposite until the path joins a road with housing R. Bear L at the swan waymark then L and R into Coldharbour Lane leading to Station Road. At All Saints Church take the path (SE) into the grounds, go past the church, and into the car park. At the stile in the corner L keep forward (SE) through a meadow by the river L. Cross through the hedge into a recreation ground, then turn sharp R to regain the car park in Marquis Lane.

NOTE: This walk can be completed from the north by parking at Someries 'Castle' G.R. 119 202 then starting at item 5, continue to 6, 7, etc.

Two shorter circular walks can also be completed as follows:

WALK A

10 Starting from the south, item 1 continue to item 4. At Peters Green, turn L along the Kimpton Road. Turn L (SW) along a footpath past the Village Hall R. At a transverse track note the housing R, cross slightly R to a path over a stile. Cross to another stile, continue (SW) with field edge L, go straight ahead following a line of trees L.

11 At a transverse path by a clump of trees, turn L (SE) along a clear track and in 200m turn R (SW) along a grassy path between fields. On reaching a large oak tree, turn L with housing R into Farrs Lane, where turn R (SW). At the B653 road cross to the road almost opposite. Continue (SW) across the river Lea, and at the end of the barbed wire fence L climb the bank at the swan waymark. Continue (SE) as in item 8.

WALK B

12 Starting from the North item 5, continue to item 8, turn L (NE) along the road under the railway bridge, and on to the road. At the B653 cross into Farrs Lane. At the end of the housing L (NE) turn L (NW) into a path. At a transverse path by a large oak tree turn R (NE). Go uphill to a transverse track where turn L (NW). On reaching a clump of trees item 10, go past and turn immediately R (NE) round them. Continue (NE) to the road at Peters Green where turn L (NW) then as in item 4 return to Someries 'Castle'.

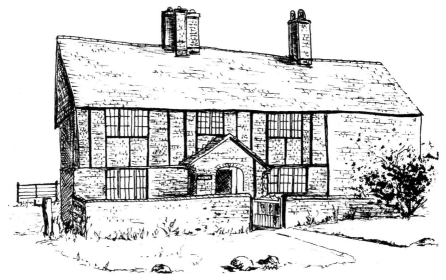

Chiltern Green Farmhouse

WALK 8

Cannons Farm, Ansells End

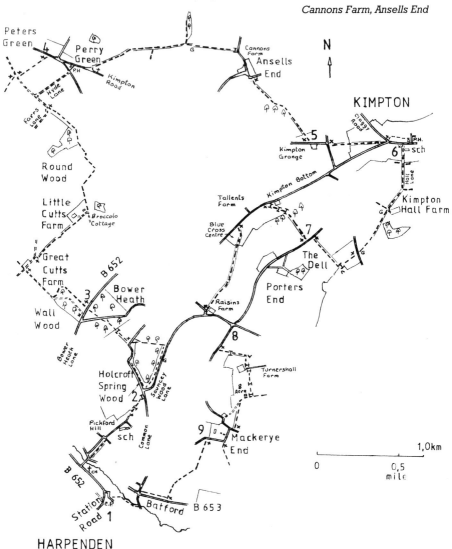

HARPENDEN

Total distance 17.0km (10.6 miles)
Shorter route 16.3km (10.1 miles)

Crown copyright reserved

26

HARPENDEN, ANSELLS END, KIMPTON, MACKERYE END

Park in Marquis Lane car park, off Station Road, Harpenden. G.R. 146 150

1 From the car park, turn L and go along Station Road (NW) past All Saints church. Turn R, cross the river Lea, and cross the Lower Luton Road. Immediately opposite, take the footpath (NE) between housing to Roundfield Avenue. Turn L then R (NE) up Pickford Hill passing a school R. At the bend, turn L (NE) along Whitings Close which leads to a path in a field with hedge R. Continue (NE) through trees, cross the stile into Common Lane.

2 Turn L (N) for a few metres, then R into Sauncey Wood Lane. Immediately bear L into the Conservancy Spinney, Holcroft Spring Wood. Bear R and follow the winding path (N) parallel with Sauncey Wood Lane R to the NE corner of the wood. In about 400m turn L along a clear track (W) to a gap in the fence L just before reaching Common Lane. Go through and cross this lane to a signpost opposite. Continue (NW) with hedge L, cross a stile and a drive into a wooded area. Keep to the same direction (NW) through the woods, cross the lane, continue through a grassy area to a 'public footpath' sign in Bower Heath Lane.

3 Cross this lane and follow a path (NW) along the boundary of Wall Wood L. Turn L round the corner of the wood (SW) to a farm access road. Turn R along this road (NW). At the intersection of paths, turn R (NE), and in 150m at the bend in the track, turn R then L at the signpost. With hedge L go down a track (NE) to Broccolo cottage. Turn L (N) round this cottage along a path between hedges for about a kilometre, emerging on to Farrs Lane. Continue (NW), and where the lane turns R, go ahead (NW) along a tarmac road. In 200m turn R (NE) at a signpost along a clear path to Peters Green.

4 Cross the Kimpton Road, turn R along it past the Bright Star P.H. R. In 400m turn L in front of the Chapel. Follow the path (E) with hedge L for about a kilometre until reaching a metal gate. Go through and continue (E) with hedge R out to the road. Turn R (SE) passing Cannons Farm L, to Ansells End. Where the road turns R, take the path R (SE) across a field, then with a hedge R for 800m to the Kimpton Road opposite Kimpton Grange.

5 Turn L along this, and in 60m at the tee junction, continue (E) on the path ahead with hedge L. This runs between houses to Claggy Road near the High Street. Cross to the path opposite (NE) between houses out to Park Lane. Turn R into the High Street at the Boot P.H. Turn R along this and in 70m turn L along Hall Lane.

6 Continue uphill (S) towards Kimpton Hall Farm. At the farm entrance go ahead (SW) through a gate, then with fence L on to a road at another gate. Cross and follow a path (SW) by a bungalow R. In 200m cross a stile, turn R (NW) along a path with hedge R to a road. Turn L (SW) for 60m to a signpost R.

7 Here turn R (NW) and with hedge L continue into a small copse. Bear L, cross the stile L (W) go down a slope diagonally crossing two more stiles to the road. Turn L (SW) along Kimpton Bottom passing Tallents Farm R. At the Blue Cross Animal Centre turn L (S) along a bridleway uphill to Raisins Farm. At the tee junction in Sauncey Wood Lane turn L (SE) to the cross roads.

8 Turn R (S) and in 250m take the path L (E), and in 150m turn R (S) round the boundary of Turnershall Farm. Cross the farm access road to the stile opposite, cross and continue (S) with hedge R over two more stiles to a transverse track. Turn R along this (W) into a lane at 'Eight Acre'. Continue (SW) along this lane, and at Holly Bush Cottage bear L (S) on to a field edge path with fence R behind Mackerye End Farm R to a road at a signpost. Turn R then in 20m L (S) passing Mackerye End House R. Follow the road round the bend (W) ignoring the signpost at the corner. In 150m there is a signpost L.

9 Take this path (S) between hedges which in 0.75km emerges on to the Wheathampstead Road. Turn R (W) and in 250m cross the road to a thatched cottage by the small industrial estate at Batford. Cross the bridge (S) over the river Lea, then turn R (W) along the path by the river bank. At the next transverse path turn L (SW) to the car park.

Alternatively In wet weather, walkers may prefer to continue along the road directly from item 7 to 8 through Porter's End.

WALK 9

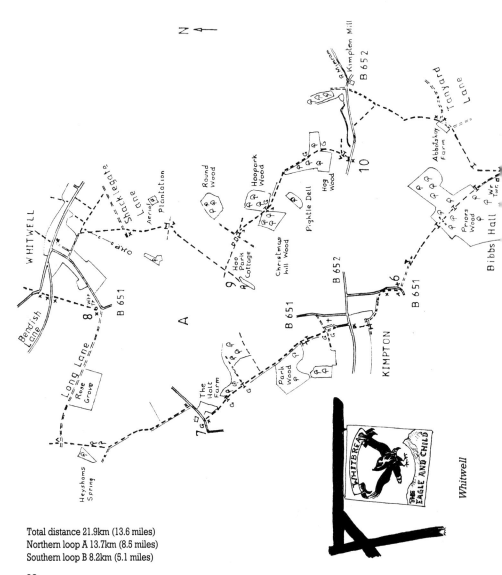

Whitwell

Total distance 21.9km (13.6 miles)
Northern loop A 13.7km (8.5 miles)
Southern loop B 8.2km (5.1 miles)

28

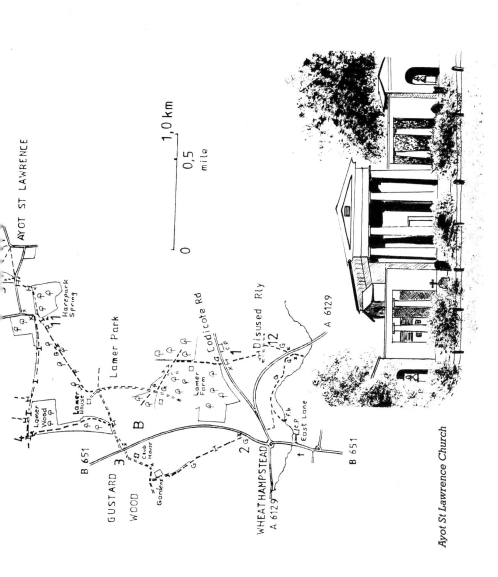

Ayot St Lawrence Church

Crown copyright reserved

29

WHEATHAMPSTEAD, WHITWELL, AYOT ST LAWRENCE

Park in car park in Codicote Road, Blackbridge site, near Lamer Park, Wheathampstead.
G.R. 185 148

1 From the car park, turn L along the Codicote Road (W) towards Wheathampstead. Continue (SW) along the Cory Wright Way to the roundabout. Turn R along Lamer Lane B651, and in 200m turn L through a gate at a signpost marked Gustard Wood.

2 Continue (NW) through a field following a line of trees, cross a stile, go through another field to a gate leading to the golf course. Continue (NW) with fence R to a crossing track at a cottage called 'Gardens'. Turn R (E) and follow this track past the club house R. Turn R again along the access road out to the Kimpton Road.

3 Cross the road, take the footpath opposite and join the access driveway to Lamer House (NE). In 200m opposite a stile R, turn L on a path through the woods (NW). This follows a fence R to the NW corner of the woods.

4 Cross the stile in the fence, turn R (E) following the edge of the wood R. Cross a stile ignoring crossing paths to the NE corner of the woods. Continue (E) crossing three more stiles with hedge L to meet a path R coming from the avenue of trees. Turn L (N) on to a track to meet a corner stile in Bibbs Hall Lane. Bear L (N) along this lane and in 250m at the road corner take the path R (E). Continue between fences crossing three stiles to the Water Tower L and the neo-classical church R.

5 Turn L (NW) round the tower to a path with woods L leading to a stile in a gate at the corner of the field. Cross and continue (NW) into the woods ahead, to a stile at the far side of the wood. On emerging from the wood continue (NW) across a field to a lone tree and on to a track at a waymark which leads to Kimpton Road B651.

6 Cross the road with care, into the field opposite to a waymarked permissive path (N) with hedge R. Go downhill past the recreation ground club house. R. Turn R (N) over a stile on to a wide track alongside the recreation ground, into Kimpton High Street. Turn R (E) and in 40m turn L up Church Lane (N). Where this lane turns R towards the church continue ahead (NW) through cottages ignoring crossing tracks. Bear R through two gates, continue (N) with fence L. Continue (NW) past a wood L, then through a small wood. Cross a field and a stile passing Holt Farm R, then bear R out to a road at a signpost

7 Turn R (NE) along this road and in 250m turn L (NW) along a signposted bridleway with hedge L. Cross two large fields. At the point where a track comes in from L, follow a short line of trees ahead (N). Continue across a field to the corner of a small wood L, then on (N) to a signpost in a transverse track Long Lane. Turn R (E) along it, go past a wood, Rose Grove R, and in about 1.25km reach a large Water Tower on a corner of the Kimpton Road B651.

8 At the Tower turn L (N) along the byway, cross Bendish Lane to the next road noting the cress beds opposite. Turn R (E) into Whitwell. Alongside the Eagle and Child P.H. turn R (SW) into Buttons Lane, go up Oldfield Rise to Bradway. Turn L along it passing a recreation ground R. At the end of the road, turn R (S) through a hedge gap. Cross under the power line and head (S) for the radio mast. In 400m is a signpost on a gravel track. A clear path continues (S) down a slope past the radio mast L. Cross a stile, go up a slope through a hedge to a transverse path.

9 Here turn L (E) with hedge L towards a large barn to meet an access road at Hoo Park Cottage. Turn L (N) for only 10m to a stile R. Cross this and head (SE) diagonally across the field to a gate and stile in Hoopark Wood. Go through, bear L and continue with wood L for 400m to a plantation R, Hog Wood. At the far corner of this, turn R (SE) alongside this wood R, go through the gate (S). Turn R over the next stile then bear L to another stile, into the Kimpton Road B652.

10 Turn L (E) with care along this busy road for 350m, and at a bend in the road, turn R (SE) along a track uphill with fence R. At the top of the hill, take the track R (S) with hedge R which leads to Abbotshay Farm and Tanyard Lane. Just beyond the farm at the bend in the lane, take the path R (SW) with hedge L. Cross a stile, go diagonally (S) across a field to another by Ayot Church. Cross this stile, turn R and take the track along the rear of the church to Bibbs Hall Lane. Turn R (W) along this lane and in 40m cross the stile (SW) at Priors Holt. Cross another stile, go down a slope to meet a transverse track in the wood Harepark Spring. Turn R (W) along this to the edge of the wood.

11 Bear L (SW) along the avenue of lime trees to Lamer House. At the house gates bear L (S) and continue along a metalled track, soon with high wire fence L. After entering woodland for only 10m turn L (E) through a large metal gate. Continue (SE) through the edge of the wood, bear L across a field by a line of trees L. At the junction with a crossing track, turn R (S) alongside a wood boundary L. Go past the derelict farm buildings R (S) to a wide track on the Codicote Road. Turn L along this to the car park R.

NOTE This walk can be completed in two shorter loops A and B, starting at item 5. Only limited parking is available at Ayot St Lawrence. G.R. 194 168.

ALTERNATIVELY

12 A more pleasant alternative at the start of the walk is to turn L from the car park, and in 100m turn L (S) at the signpost on a track along the infill area L to the disused railway track. Turn L (E) along this, and in 40m turn R (S) along a lane down to the underpass below the Cory Wright Way. At the signpost R, turn sharp R (NW) along a path parallel to the road. Continue (W) through two gates with views of the river Lea. At the housing boundary, the path turns R (N) through a small industrial area to the Cory Wright Way. Here turn L to the roundabout in item 1. This increases the length of the walk by 1.5km.

Ayot Old Church

31

WALK 10

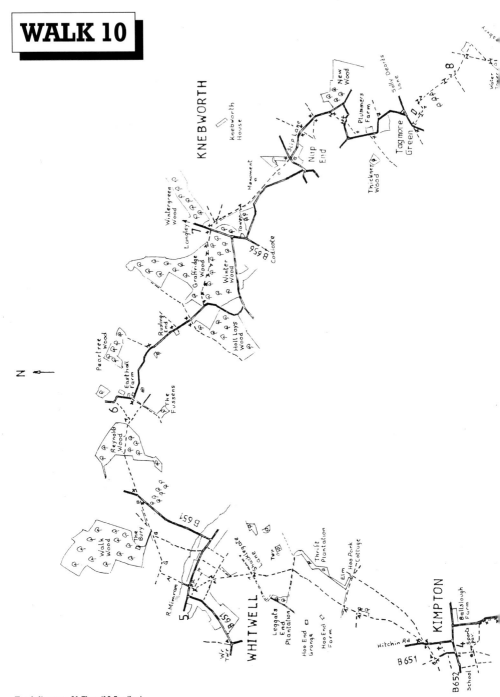

Total distance 21.7km (13.5 miles)

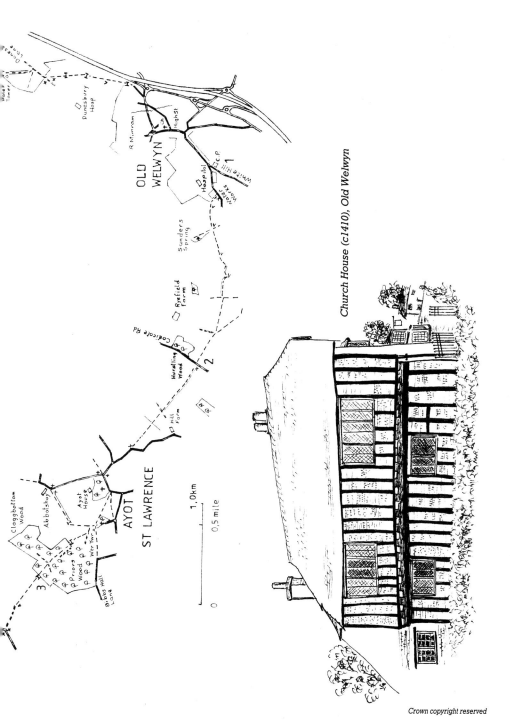

Church House (c1410), Old Welwyn

Crown copyright reserved

33

OLD WELWYN, KIMPTON, WHITWELL, KNEBWORTH PARK

WALK

10

Park in public car park at the bottom of White Hill, Old Welwyn. G.R. 227 157.

1 From the car park, walk down the hill (NE) for 30m to the tee junction. Turn sharp L (SW) along the Ayot St Peter road past the hospital and water works R. At the end of the iron railings, turn R (NW) at the signpost, climb the bank, and follow the fence R to the corner. Turn sharp L (W), and aim for the trees in the distance, cross the farm track. Continue along the field edge with trees L (W). Go through the gap in the hedge, follow the clear path (NW) into a bridleway downhill to the Codicote road.

2 Cross the road at the signpost, and follow the bridleway with hedge L (NW). Cross the track leading to Hill Farm, and continue (NW) across the field to the road. Continue along the road (NW) ignore the road turning R. After about 150m enter the bridleway R (N) by the signpost, go past The Manor House L, to Abbotsbury. Turn L (SW) at the signpost then with hedge L continue to a stile. Cross the field (S) towards the water tower. At the fence turn 120 degrees R (NW) alongside it, to the corner stile. Enter the wood (NW) along a well marked path to a stile in the far boundary.

3 Continue across the field (NW) towards a lone tree, into a track. Here turn slightly L (NW) along the track to a road bend. Take care in crossing this road to the signpost opposite, climb the bank and bear R (N) along the permissive path with hedge R. Bear L (W) at the waymark, past the sports pavilion R. Turn R (N) alongside the playing field R. Leave the field by the track which emerges on to Kimpton High Street.

4 Turn R along the High Street and in 40m turn L into Church Lane. Continue (N) up hill past the church (R) into a path between cottages. At the open fields, turn R (NE) alongside a cottage wall (R) to the road. Turn L up this road for 30m to the signpost at a road bend. Enter the track R and in a few metres bear L along the path running diagonally across the field (NNE) aiming for the L edge of the copse in the distance. Go alongside this copse (NE) to a gap in a crossing hedge. Go through and continue (NE) straight across the next field down to a stile. Cross this, bear L (N) past the radio mast R. Cross the next farm track called Shacklegate Lane. Follow the hedge R (N) to Whitwell playing fields. Cross these diagonally (N) to the tarmac path down to the road L (W) to housing in Whitwell. Turn R (N) down Oldfield Rise, follow the track between housing to Buttons Lane alongside the Eagle and Child P.H.

5 Cross Whitwell High Street and continue down then up the lane (NE) into a track. Bear R (E) at the tee junction and in 100m enter a field R at a gate. Go diagonally (NE) across the field to another gate. Continue along a track and in 40m at a signpost bear R (NE) through another gate down across a meadow towards a lodge at the corner of a walled garden. Go through trees to the road. Turn L and in 20m turn R at a signpost up a track into Reynolds Wood. Continue (E) through the wood ignoring paths on L. At the edge of the wood bear L (NE) on to a path past farm buildings R to a road corner.

6 Turn R (S) along this road and follow it around Easthall Farm L. Continue (SE) along this road past three signposts L to the boundary of Graffridge Wood. In a few metres turn L on a forest track (E) which is well waymarked. In about 500m is a road B656 which is crossed to a signpost opposite in a copse. Enter this, bear R to a ladder stile into Knebworth Park.

7 Follow the fence R (SE), cross two more ladder stiles, then a high stile to the road. Cross and continue opposite (SE) along Slip Lane for 500m. Take the third signposted path R (SW) cross the stile, through the hedge gap, and head diagonally across the field (SW). Continue across a lane and the next field to join another lane. Turn L (S) go past Plummer Farm L to Tagmore Green. At the tee junction bear R (SW) and in 300m turn L over a stile at the corner of a chainlink fence. Continue (SE) with fence R through two fields to a field corner. Turn L (NE) at a waymark, and in 100m turn R over two stiles (SE).

8 Continue (SE) across another field and cross a third stile, bear R with hedge R to a field corner. Turn R (S) over a stile towards the water tower. Go past the tower R into a lane. Bear L (SE) and in 40m turn R (S) along an unmade road for 100m. At the signpost L cross a stile (S) into fields, go down the slope towards Old Welwyn. Cross three stiles (S) and emerge into a road behind the Clock Restaurant. Cross the road with care to Church Street signed Welwyn shops. Go downhill (SW) to St Marys Church. At the tee junction turn L (S) along the High Street which leads to White Hill and the car park.

*Spanish Chestnut
in Knebworth Park*

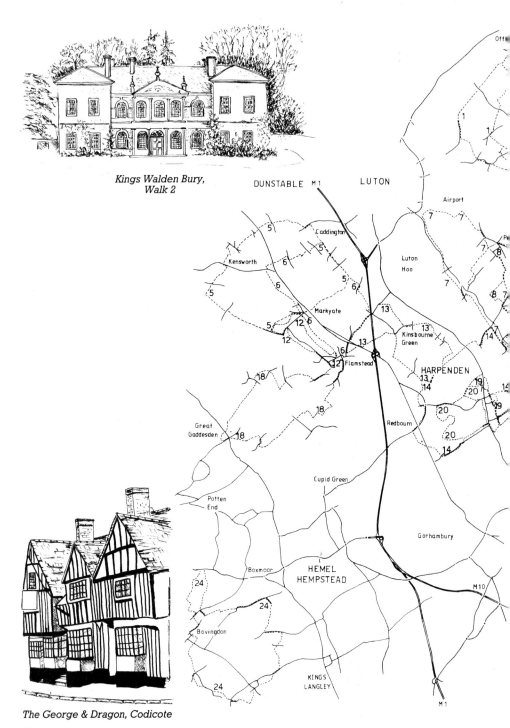

Kings Walden Bury,
Walk 2

The George & Dragon, Codicote

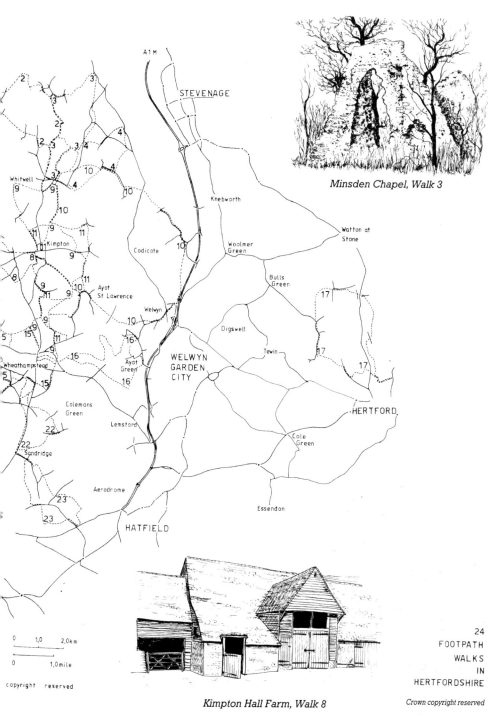

Minsden Chapel, Walk 3

Kimpton Hall Farm, Walk 8

copyright reserved

Crown copyright reserved

24
FOOTPATH
WALKS
IN
HERTFORDSHIRE

WALK 11

N ↑

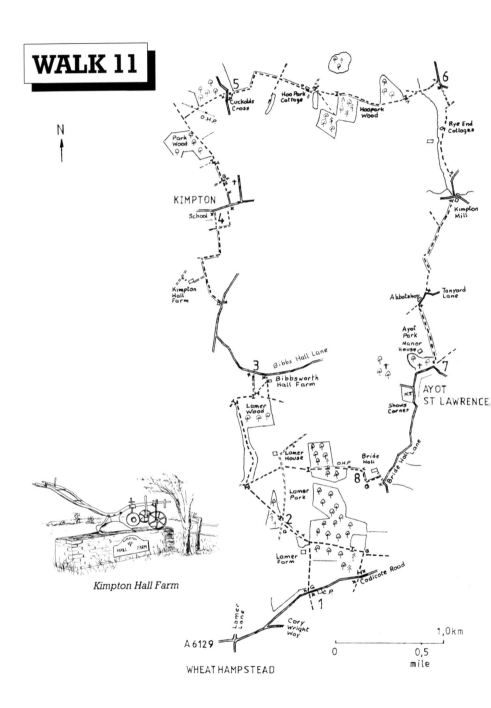

Kimpton Hall Farm

Total distance 14.8km (9.2 miles)

Crown copyright reserve

38

WHEATHAMPSTEAD, KIMPTON, AYOT ST LAWRENCE

Park in car park in Codicote Road, Blackbridge site, near Lamer Park, Wheathampstead. G.R. 185 148

1 From the car park turn R along Codicote Road and in 400m, take the path L at signpost. Walk (N) with conifer wood L, and at the corner of the wood turn L through the deer gate. Continue (W) across the field into another conifer wood. At a transverse path with the derelict buildings of Lamer Farm L, bear R (NW) across a field into a wood. Go through another deer gate on to a driveway.

2 Turn R (N) and in 20m L (NW) over a stile into a wood. On emerging from the wood continue (NW) across a field, heading for the L corner of the wood, to a stile on the access road. Cross this and take the path opposite (N) into Lamer Wood. Follow this to a squeeze exit at the boundary of the wood. Turn R (E) along boundary of the wood R, and in 200m turn L (N) just before a stile. Then with hedge R pass the farm buildings R into Bibbs Hall Lane.

3 Turn L (NW) to a tee junction where turn R. In 300m turn L (N) on to a signed track to Kimpton Hall Farm. Ignore the track L, continue with hedge L on a concrete track to a transverse hedge. Turn R (E) alongside this hedge R to the corner of the field, go through the gap in the hedge, turn L and follow the hedge L (N). At the transverse path, turn R and in 90m turn L (N). Continue down to Kimpton High Street.

4 Turn R and in 40m turn L (N) along Church Lane. Just before the bend in the lane, bear L at the pipe rail gap continue (N) along a path across a grassy area between housing. Cross a transverse track through two gates, go up the field path (N) with fence L. At the stile, cross and continue (NW) with a wood L. Go past Park Wood and in 200m turn R along a grass track (NE). Cross under a power line to meet the boundary of the wood L and go out to the road at Cuckolds Cross.

5 At the road turn R and in 10m at a signpost turn L. Walk round the house garden, continue (E) with hedge L. Follow round the field along the hedge L, cross a transverse path to the large barn at Hoo Park Cottages. At the driveway turn L and in 15m R over a waymarked stile. Continue straight across the field (E), ignore the diagonal path (SE), to reach a stile at the corner of Hoo Park Wood R. Continue (E) alongside this wood R then a hedge R. Soon the path leads to another wood L with a stile and waymark at the far corner. Cross and bear L down the field to a gate into a driveway. Bear R along this drive, cross the bridge over the river Mimram to a road junction.

6 Turn R (S) along this and in 20m bear R at the bridleway sign. Continue past Rye End Cottages R, and farm R, along the river valley to meet a lane at a bend. Continue (S) past watercress beds R, down to the road at Kimpton Mill. Cross the road to the signed path opposite. Go uphill (SW) with hedge R to Tanyard Lane and Abbotshay. Bear R along the lane and in 100m bear L along a signed bridleway (S). Go past the Manor House to the road at Ayot St Lawrence village.

7 At the road junction turn R (SW) pass the ruined church R and follow round to G. B. Shaws Corner, a National Trust property. Fork L along the road (S) for 900m to Bride Hall R. At the path sign go up the steps and cross the stile. Walk to the brick wall, follow it, go through a gate at the corner of the wall. Turn R (NW) with fence R and at the fence corner turn L (W) along a wide grassy track.

8 Continue (W) through the wood following the power line. Cross the stile, and continue across a field into the access road near Lamer House. Turn L (S) along this gravel road with deer fence L. At the deer gate L (item 1) go through, continue (SE) along a track through the wood, then diagonally (SE) across a field. At the edge of the wood, turn R (S) past the derelict farm buildings R, go out through the gate into Codicote Road. Turn L along this and in 80m turn R into the car park.

WALK 12

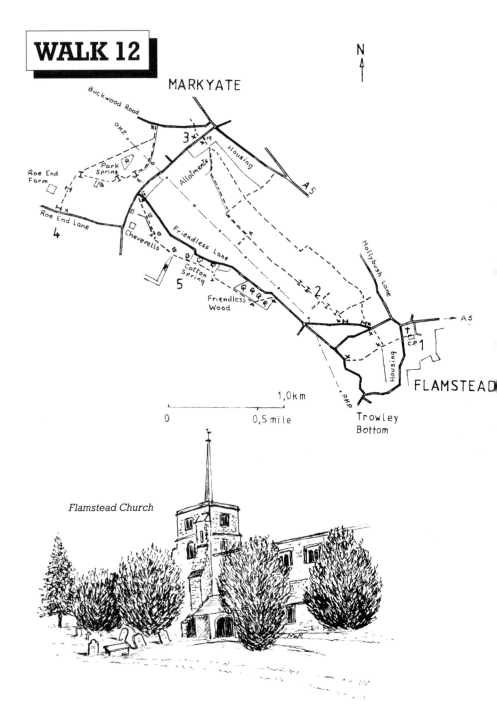

Flamstead Church

Total distance 8.5km (5.3 miles)

Crown copyright reserved

40

FLAMSTEAD, MARKYATE, CHEVERELLS

Park in the car park at Flamstead Village Hall, Church Lane. Flamstead. G.R. 079 145

1 Leave the car park (W) along the churchyard path, passing the church R. Cross Trowley Hill Road, go diagonally L to the signed path opposite. Continue (W) on a path between housing for 150m to a transverse path along a field edge. Turn R (NW) to meet a road tee junction. Take the road opposite, bearing slightly L (W). In about 200m at the second footpath sign R cross the stile. Follow the fence R (NW) to a double stile having a hinged topmost bar. Continue (NW) across the field to a second similar stile.

2 Cross the farm track, continue (NW) to a stile in a hedge marked by white posts. Cross into a large field, and go ahead (NW) across it aiming for the hedge corner which soon becomes visible in the distance. At this corner a clear track continues (NW) with hedge L. Follow round a short R and L to allotments. Keep to the allotments fence L (NW). At the play area, take the L fork downhill to the road alongside number 19.

3 Turn L (W) along the road, and in 10m turn R (NW) through metal gates on a path through housing. Cross a road and go past the Baptist Chapel R, out to Buckwood Road. Turn L (W) and in 200m reach the end of the housing. At the signpost marked Roe End Lane, turn L (S) and go uphill with hedge and housing L towards a power pylon L. Follow round the field corners (W) cross two stiles, go past a metal gate L. At the third stile, cross and turn L (S) alongside a hedge L, past Roe End Farm R. This leads to a stile into Roe End Lane.

4 Turn L (E) along this lane for 600m to a tee junction opposite the house 'Cheverells'. Turn L (NE) along Pickford Hill, and in 200m turn R (SE) onto a road signposted Flamstead. In 20m turn R through a signed swing gate. Continue (SE) diagonally across a field to a second gate, on the left of two. In a further 300m go through a third gate with fence R. Continue (S) through a fourth gate at the end of a woodland strip R. Go across a field (SE) to another gate, on the R of two, in a wood called Cotton Spring.

5 Continue forward with wood L, follow round a short R and L, do not turn L towards farm buildings, follow the waymark ahead (SE). Continue with hedge L then the boundary of Friendless Wood L. In a further 200m at a waymark, turn L (E) on a path through the wood to Friendless Lane (see note). Turn R along the lane (SE). At the crossroads go ahead (SE) under the power line. Pass another road junction L and as the road begins to go downhill, turn L (E) at a footpath sign. Continue (E) towards Flamstead Church, retrace the path between housing in item 1 to return to the churchyard and the car park.

Note. A Mr Frindles owned land in this area in the mid 19th century. It seems likely that the writing of this name became corrupted to 'Friendless'.

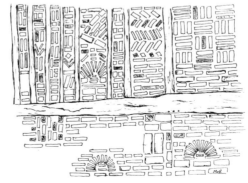

End wall of cottage in Markyate

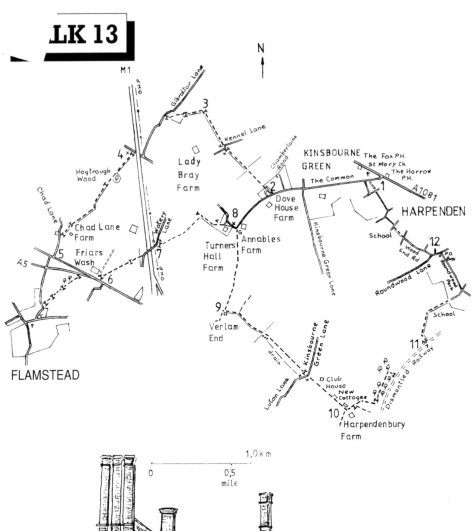

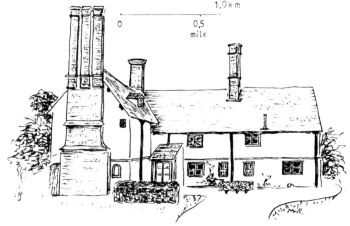

Turners Hall Farm

Total distance 13.5km (8.4 miles)
Shorter route 12.9km (8.0 miles)

Crown copyright reserved

KINSBOURNE GREEN, FLAMSTEAD, ANNABLES

ark at Kinsbourne Green, near the junction of 'The Common' and Luton Road A1081 oppo-
te The Harrow public house. G.R. 115 161

From the road junction, walk (W) along 'The Common' on the grassy verge L past attractive houses for 0.75km. Cross Kinsbourne Green Lane. Continue (W) past Chamberlains road R, and in 200m turn R (NW) along a path between gardens.

Beyond these gardens continue (NW) on a grassy track, through a transverse wire fence. Continue (NW) with wire fence L, cross a stile into Kennel Lane. Turn R and immediately L at the signpost along a path with hedge L (NW). Just before the next stile in a field corner, avoid a waterlogged area by keeping to the hedge L. Cross the stile and turn L (W).

Follow the ditch L along the field edge, cross a stile into a meadow. Go diagonally R (W) aiming to the L of the power pylon. Cross a stile into Gibraltar Lane, turn L (SW) along it. At the end of the lane, turn R and go under the motorway.

On emerging from the underpass, climb the roadside bank L, cross the stile and continue (SW) with wire fence L. Go past Hogtrough Wood L, follow the hedge or fence L, go under the power line into a paddock. Cross the stile into Chad Lane by the farm, turn L go down to the end of the lane.

Turn R (NW) along old Watling Street, and in 10m turn L (S) down to the A5. Cross with care and continue (S) uphill into Flamstead Village. Here are two inns which provide food, also interesting alms-houses and a church. To continue, retrace your steps down the lane (N) by the telephone box. Cross the stile R by the allotments and continue (NE) with hedge R. In 100m cross a stile with hedge L. Enter a wood and in a few metres continue along a field edge to another stile. Bear R towards the Shell filling station, climb the bank through the hedge gap, turn R (SE) passing the garage and Watling Street Cafe L.

Cross the road, and at the far end of the garage forecourt cross the stile low down, behind the plant-ed edge. Cross the field (NE) heading just to R of the power pylon. Cross another stile, head for the pylon, turn L along the macadam path onto Watery Lane bridge over the M1.

At the far end of the bridge, cross the stile R into a field. Follow the path (NE) across the field. At the hedge corner waymark, turn (SE) and follow the hedge R towards the large brick barn. Continue (E) past the farm R, cross the farm access road and paddock to a signpost in Annables Lane.

In a few metres where the lane turns L, turn R (S) through metal gates to a farm track. Ignore the transverse path, continue along a broad gravel track (S).

At Verlam End, turn L (E) before the house along a grassy path with hedge R. At a transverse hedge near the beehives, continue ahead (SE) aiming for a group of trees just to R of a building with a single chimney stack. Cross a stile into Luton Lane. Cross the road to the bridleway opposite. Continue (SE) passing Redbourn golf club house and New Cottages L.

Pass a large barn L, and just in front of the entrance to Harpendenbury Farm, turn L (NE) past a barn R. Where the track turns R, go forward (NE) over a stile into a paddock with fields L. Cross a stile L (N) into a woodland with golf course on L. On emerging from the wood, turn R (E) at the waymark keeping to the edge of the golf course R. In about 100m turn sharp R (E) cross a stile. In a further 50m at a tee junction with the Nicky Way, a disused railway track, turn L (NE) along it. In about 450m at a power pole turn L (NW) at a waymark.

Bear R, pass a gated paddock, and continue (N) past Roundwood School R between housing. At the first cross road, turn L (NW) along Roundwood Park. Ignore side roads, continue to a post box at a tee junction. Turn L (W) into Roundwood Lane, then the second turning R (NW) Wood End Road.

Continue to Wood End School, then (NW) along a path with the School boundary L. At the tee junction turn R into Tuffnells Way, then L into Crosspaths. Bear R into Shepherds Way. At the bend in the road keep forward (N) along a path between housing to meet the Common and the car park.

ematively If you do not wish to visit Flamstead Village at item 5, turn L along Old Watling Street directly to
e garage item 6.

WALK 14

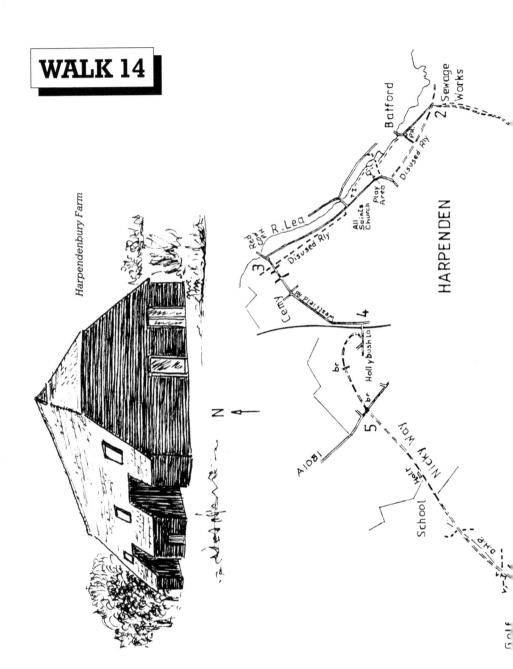

Harpendenbury Farm

N

HARPENDEN

Batford

Sewage Works

R.Lea

Disused Rly

Disused Rly

Red Cow P.H.

Play Area

All Saints Church

P.H.

Cemy

West Field La

2

3

4

5

br

br

Hollybush La

A1081

Nicky Way

Hatching Green

School

DWP

Golf

Total distance 16.1km (10.0 miles)

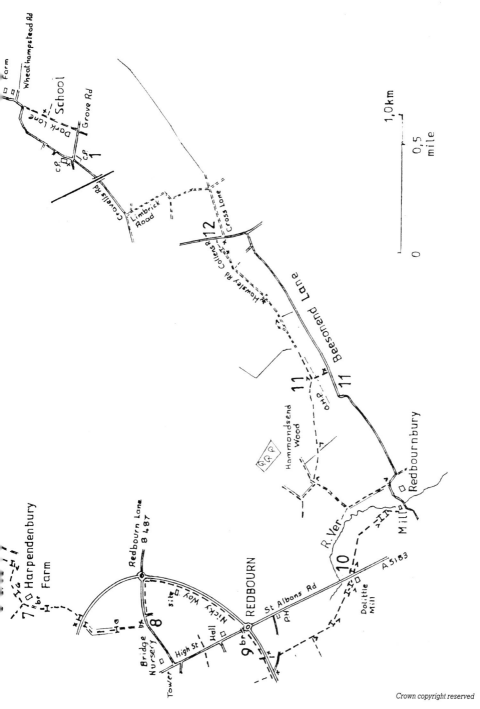

Crown copyright reserved

45

CIRCULAR WALK ROUND HARPENDEN

Part of Lea Valley walk and the Nicky Way.

Park in the Somerfield car park behind supermarket in Southdown. Entrance is in Southdown Road opposite Walkers Road. G.R. 144 133.

1 Leave the car park at the furthest point from the entrance into Piggottshill Lane between shops. Turn R and immediately L (E) into Grove Road, then first L (N) into Dark Lane. Pass school buildings R. At a transverse row of concrete bollards turn R, and L into a footpath (N) passing allotment gardens R. Continue forward (N) with housing L and at a major road turn R to a mini roundabout. Cross and continue (N) into a lane with housing L and farm buildings R. Just beyond a wide iron gate R enter a woodland path parallel to the lane, and continue (N) with sewage works plant R and L.

2 Walk under the disused railway bridge, turn L along Marquis Lane to the Marquis of Granby P.H. Alternatively, for the energetic, climb the bank to the R of the bridge, turn L over the bridge, and at a pole barrier, turn R and descend to Marquis Lane. At the P.H. turn R (NE) and shortly L (NW) into a path alongside the river Lea R. Continue with park L and river R noting the picturesque weir R. One can cross the river to view the weir, then cross back at the far end of the path (NW). Continue alongside a narrow section of the river R. Cross a stile into the car park at All Saints church. Cross the front of the church into Station Road, and at the junction keep forward L into Coldharbour Lane. Within a few metres enter a metalled path L then immediately R on to the old railway path (NW) running parallel to Coldharbour Lane.

3 On reaching a main road look R to notice the Red Cow P.H. but turn L (SW) along Westfield Road. Pass Harpenden Cemetery R continue alongside Thameslink railway R.

4 At Holly Bush Lane turn R, cross the railway bridge, turn R again into a path which descends a deep stairway to the commencement of the 'Nicky Way' (SW). This is the route of the former rail link between the main line and Hemel Hempstead.

5 In about 0.5km this path crosses the A1081 St Albans to Luton road where if you need shops or restaurants you may descend steps R at the far of the bridge, walk under it to enter Harpenden town. On returning, ascend these steps to the Nicky Way and continue (SW). After crossing a raised transverse path, notice the remains of a railway Halt platform with a signal arm R. Pass a school R and garden nursery L. Keep forward at the first transverse path, but at the second turn R (W).

6 In a few metres cross a waymarked stile in the corner of hedges. Continue (W) with trees L and golf course R. Just before the end of the wooded area, turn L (S) into it by a waymark post, and follow a clear path with golf course R. At a waymarked stile, cross and turn R (W) into a paddock, alongside the golf course boundary R. Cross the next stile by a metal gate into a track and keep forward (SW).

Redbournbury Mill and Ford

7 At a transverse track note the ancient but now refurbished barn L in Harpendenbury Farm. Cross the steel footbridge opposite (S) on to the golf course, bear L (S) with grass mound L. Keep to the L edge of the golf course which is marked by red topped white posts. Cross a stile into a meadow, keep forward (SW) to a signposted stile at the Redbourn by-pass. Cross this and the stile opposite, and keep forward (SW) along a wide grassy strip between wire fences. The way bends L (S). Cross a stile by a gate into a track to reach Harpenden Lane.

8 Cross this road, turn L (E) towards the roundabout along the roadside path. At the roundabout, turn R (S) into the Nicky Way as it runs parallel with the by-pass (A5183). Go past the entrance to the modern travellers site R. On approaching the bridge over Redbourn High Street the walk continues forward (SW) over it.

Alternatively if you wish to visit the pleasant village of Redbourn do not cross the bridge, but turn R and descend the steps to the road. Turn R (NW) to the village where there are refreshments. Toilets are available at the village hall car park. Return to the bridge go up the steps and continue forward (SW) over the High Street.

9 In 250m where a path enters from housing R, turn immediately L by a low level transformer on to a grassy track. On reaching the by-pass cross immediately, ignoring the footpath sign L and enter a metalled lane. Shortly, by a private gated entrance, turn R in front of a wooden fence at the Ver Valley Walk waymark. Keep forward (S) at a single oak tree to a stile with hedge R (SE). Usually there are horses in this field but do not attempt to make contact with them. Cross two stiles at Dolittle Mill on to Watling Street A5183 an old Roman Road.

10 Cross this road and the stile opposite, still follow the Ver Valley signs. At a transverse track cross two stiles and enter a hedged grassy track alongside Redbournbury Mill L. On reaching the farm road, turn L (E) in front of the mill continue (NE) over two footbridges past Redbournbury Farm R. Where the road bends R, turn L (NW) on to a wide track, and in 500m turn R (NE) into a rising track. In 400m by an oak tree and waymark, bear R (E) across a field, then go through a waymarked gap in the hedge.

11 Continue forward (E) and at the top of the slope, keep forward by a waymark past a power post R and housing L. Ignore the parallel roadway L, continue on a path between fences. At the far end cross the road into Hawsley Road, continue ahead into Collens Road, Locate and cross a stile within the hedge, go ahead to the main road A1081. A bollard just S of the junction provides a safe crossing of this very busy road.

12 Turn R then L into Cross Lane. At a cross roads with posting box R, turn L (N). At the tee junction by Limbrick Hall turn R, then turn L at the next junction (N). At the third tee junction turn R (E) by a posting box into Cravells Road to return to Southdown and the car park.

Redbournbury Farm

WALK 15

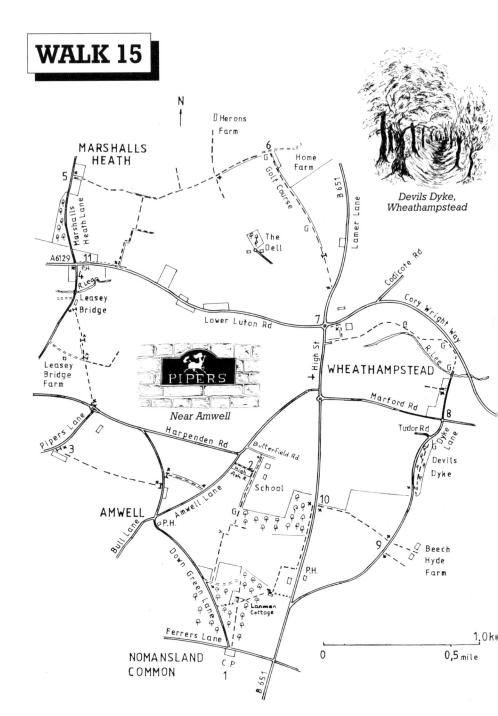

Devils Dyke,
Wheathampstead

N

Herons Farm

MARSHALLS
HEATH

5

Marshalls Heath Lane

Golf Course

6

Home Farm

G

B 651

Lamer Lane

A6129 11

P.H.

4

R.Lea

Leasey
Bridge

The
Dell

Lower Luton Rd

7

High St

Codicote Rd

Cory Wright Way

R.Lee

G
G

WHEATHAMPSTEAD

Leasey
Bridge
Farm

Pipers Lane

PIPERS

Near Amwell

Harpenden Rd

3

Butterfield Rd.

Marford Rd

8

Tudor Rd

Dyke Lane

Devils
Dyke

2

High Ash R

School

10

9

Beech
Hyde
Farm

AMWELL

P.H.

Bull Lane

Amwell Lane

G

Down Green Lane

P.H.

Lanman
Cottage

Ferrers Lane

NOMANSLAND
COMMON

C.P.

1

B 651

1,0 km

0   0,5 mile

Total distance 11.3km (7.0 miles)

Crown copyright reserve

48

CIRCULAR WALK AROUND WHEATHAMPSTEAD

Park in car park on Nomansland Common opposite junction of Down Green Lane with Ferrers Lane. G.R. 172 123.

1 Cross the road (N) and go up Down Green Lane. After about 300m, take the second lane R, turn immediately L at a signpost along a path (N) between hedges. Continue to a wood, turn R at a wooden sign, go round the corner of the field. Go through a hedge gap R then turn L to follow this hedge L (N). After 20m turn R into a woodland strip and immediately L (N) to a pipe rail barrier at a school boundary.

2 At the housing, take the first path L through a pipe rail barrier into High Ash Road. Go along this (NW) to its junction with Amwell Lane, along which turn L (SW). In about 250m at a signpost take the path R (W) to a stile in Down Green Lane. Turn L (S) and in about 150m at a signpost opposite Weavers Cottage take the fenced path R (SW) to Pipers Lane.

3 Turn R along this lane (NE) to meet the Harpenden/Wheathampstead road. Cross and at signpost take the path opposite (N) which joins a track near Leasey Bridge Farm. Cross the transverse track to a stile, and follow the swan waymark (N) with hedge L. Continue diagonally across a field to a bungalow 'Little Croft' into Leasey Bridge Lane. Turn R along this lane, cross the river pausing to admire the picturesque setting. Continue to the Lower Luton Road by the Cherry Tree public house.

4 Cross the road and continue up Marshalls Heath Lane (N). After about 100m take the path on R in the woods parallel to this road.

5 In about 600m at the bridleway signpost R, turn R (E) between houses, and continue across open fields. This clear track continues to a four way signpost just S of Herons Farm. Cross and continue (E) along a path with hedge and golf course R.

6 Cross the track which enters the golf course, turn R at the signpost (SE) go through the gate, follow a hedge then a fence L, down to another gate. Continue (SE) over a stile, down through a gate to the Kimpton/Wheathampstead road. Cross the road, turn R (S) go down to the roundabout.

7 Cross at the traffic island, and turn L along the Cory Wright Way (E). In about 10m turn R at the bridleway sign (S) passing a disused factory L. In about 40m turn L (E) along a transverse bridleway. Soon this gives good views of the river R. After passing through two gates, the path continues with wooden railings on each side alongside the main road. It then meets a gravel lane, crosses the river Lea and continues (S) as Sheepcote Lane to the Marford Road.

8 Cross this road, continue (S) up Dyke Lane. In 70m opposite the junction with Tudor Road at a footpath sign L enter Devils Dyke. Continue (S) to the far end, turn sharp R and retrace your steps (N) for 40m along a path leading out to a lane. Turn L (S) and in 100m is Beech Hyde Farm.

9 Turn R at the signpost opposite the farm entrance, take the clear path across a field (NW). Continue with housing fence R to the Sandridge/Wheathampstead Road.

10 Cross the road B651 with care and take the path L (S) parallel with the road. In about 400m turn R then L following the boundary of a small wood and the kennels L. Go between the pavilion and the toilets (W) bear L along a grassy path through the woods (SW). At Lanman Cottage continue (SW) through the wood to the car park.

Alternatively:

1 At item 4 cross the road, turn R along a path. In 600m at an access road just before a brick wall is a signpost. Turn L (N) and follow the hedge R. At the top of the enclosed garden after a short R and L, continue (N) on the field path. This meets a bridleway along which turn R to item 6.

WALK 16

N

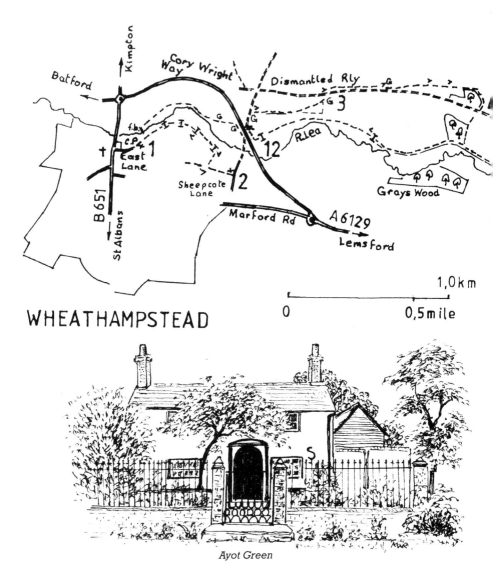

WHEATHAMPSTEAD

1,0km

0   0,5mile

Ayot Green

Total distance 14.5km (9.0 miles)
Shorter route 11.7km (7.3 miles)

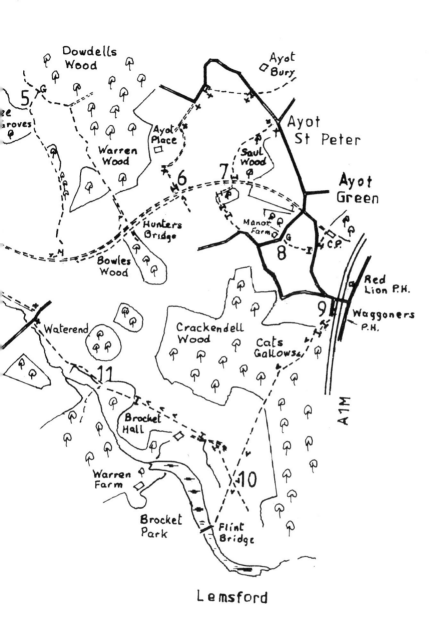

Dowdells Wood

Ayot Bury

Ayot Place

Ayot St Peter

Saul Wood

Ayot Green

Warren Wood

5

6

7

8

Hunters Bridge

Manor Farm

C.P.

Bowles Wood

Red Lion P.H.

9

Waggoners P.H.

Waterend

Crackendell Wood

Cats Gallows

11

A1M

Brocket Hall

Warren Farm

10

Brocket Park

Flint Bridge

Lemsford

Crown copyright reserved

51

WHEATHAMPSTEAD, AYOT ST PETER, BROCKET PARK

WALK

16

Park in public car park in East Lane, behind the Bull Inn, Wheathampstead. G.R. 178 141.

1 From the car park, turn L into East Lane (NE), bear L into Meads Lane, which soon becomes an asphalt track. Go through a gateway to a three way signpost, follow the sign 'Sheepcote Lane 1/2m' ahead (E) with hedge R. Where the hedge bends R, continue ahead (SE) into a fenced path with paddock L. Cross a stile into a small field with hedge R, continue (SE) to another stile, cross a third stile by a gate into a larger field. At the field corner in the hedge R cross a fourth stile, turning R (SW) into a fenced path to a waymarked tee junction of paths. Turn L (E) with fence L and allotments R, go between posts into a narrow path between houses into Sheepcote Lane.

2 Turn L (N) along this lane past farm buildings R, cross the river Lea, and continue under the Cory Wright Way. In about 100m by an iron gate, turn R in front of it through a gap by another iron gate into a field path with hedge R. Continue (E) through a gap to a second field, ignore the waymarked stile R. Here the path bears L (NE) diagonally across the field to a gate in the far corner. It is permissible to go ahead (E) to the far corner, then to turn L (N) uphill with hedge R to reach the same gate. Go through this gate, down the slope to the dismantled railway track called the 'Ayot Green Way'.

3 Cross this track, bear L for a few metres to a bridleway sign opposite, where turn R (E) along a fenced path which climbs alongside the track (R). This path descends (E) into a valley, through a gate at a wood corner R. Note the blue waymark, go uphill across a field (E) to another waymark, into a further field with edge of wood R. Turn R (S) round the boundary of this wood to rejoin the track.

4 Turn L (E) along the track for 500m to a waymarked path by a bench seat L. Take this path (E) up to a wide gravel crossing track at a bridge. Turn L (N) on this track uphill past a corner of a wood R. Note the wide views S. Continue into a path (N) following a line of oaks past a small wood R. Continue (N) across a field towards a wood corner L, then follow the edge of this wood L. The path turns R (NE) with hedge L, to meet a bridleway at a tee junction by a double gate.

5 Turn R (SE) along this bridleway with the edge of the wood L. After 600m enter the wood for 150m. On emerging from the wood, go ahead to a gap L in the hedge, and continue (SE) along a field edge with hedge R. Ignore the steps R, go under the railway bridge called Hunters Bridge, and immediately turn L (NE) following the foot of the railway embankment L. In 350m turn L (NW) over a stile near a power line junction. Cross the railway track to a stile opposite near a power post, on to a field path (NW).

6 Cross the field to meet a narrow service road at a bend, turn R (E) at the signpost. Follow this road past rhododendrons to a tee junction where turn R (NE). Leave this drive road through a gateway with lodge R into a road at a bend. Continue along the road (NE) for 100m, turn R to cross a signposted stile in a hedge near a large oak. Cross the field (E) to a signposted stile in the hedge opposite out to a road. Turn R (SE) along the road and just before the road junction turn R (SW) into a signposted path into a wood. Avoid a fork L near a garden gate, continue downhill (SW) with edge of wood R, emerging over a stile on to the railway track again.

7 Cross the track and the stile opposite (S). Cross the field (S) to the power pylon by the wood. Turn R (SW) follow the edge of the wood L to the next pylon at the wood corner. Turn L (S) and follow the downhill path with wood L. Near the bottom of the slope cross a stile in a hedge L and follow a fence R (S). Cross this fence at another stile into a hedged uphill path (S). Go between posts, bear R and immediately L to a road at Manor Farm Cottage. Follow this road (SE) and at the tee junction turn L to the entrance gate of Manor Farm L. Notice ahead a waymarked horse chestnut tree with tall hedge R. This is Ayot Little Green.

8 Bear R (SE) to a bungalow named 'Gayton' into a narrow path with a gate marked 'no bridleway'. Go through into a field with wooden fence L. Turn R (E) to follow the hedge R down to a stile at a road. Turn R (S) along the road to Ayot Green bear L (SE) past attractive cottages, to a bridge over the A1(M).

9 Here a detour to the Red Lion may be made by crossing the bridge and turning L for a few metres. Immediately before crossing the bridge, turn R (S) into Brickwall Close, once part of the old Great North Road. Opposite the 'Waggoners Inn' L, cross a stile R (SW) into a fenced path. Cross a second stile (SW) into Brocket Park with lodge L. Follow the waymarks through conifers, avoiding paths which fork L or R, continue (SW) up a slope on to a large golf course. Take the gravel track ahead (SW) across the course heading for the edge of woodland.

10 At the estate road, cross and turn sharp R (NW) into a fenced path with woodland L. Cross a stile, and the estate road to the stile opposite. Continue uphill (NW) with views of Brocket Hall and the lake S. This well waymarked path leads to a stile in a wood boundary ahead. Go through the wood (NW) along an embankment with iron railings L, then descend steeply to a crossing track. (A short detour L leads to a flint bridge over the river Lea in pleasant woodland surroundings).

11 Cross the track continue (NW) along a path first with fence L then R. This follows the river L and emerges on to a road at Waterend with ford L. Turn R, then in a few metres turn L (NW) opposite the large Elizabethan House. This gravel bridleway follows the river with hedge L. In 500m at a bend, continue ahead (W) through fields onto a short enclosed path. Cross the stile into water meadows (W). Continue to a signposted stile by the Cory Wright Way.

12 Follow the fenced path down a slope (NW) through the iron gate. Soon bear L into a hedge gap to a permissive path following the river L. Cross the footbridge L and retrace the outward route along Meads Lane, and East Lane to the car park.

Alternatively: This walk can be shortened by keeping on the old railway track from item 3 to 7, but the walk as described is more pleasant.

Waterend House

WALK 17

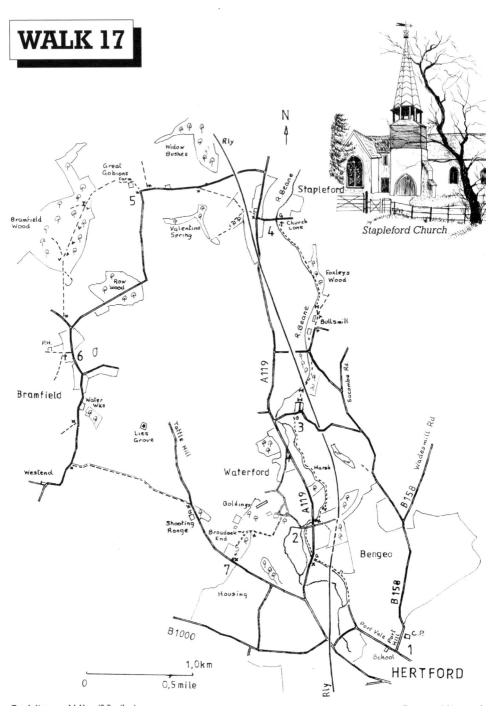

Stapleford Church

Total distance 14.1km (8.8 miles)

Crown copyright reserved

54

HERTFORD, WATERFORD, STAPLEFORD, BRAMFIELD, BROADOAK

A riverside walk from Hertford.

Park in the public car park at the Hartham Swimming Pool with access from Port Hill B158 (Bengeo Road), Hertford. G.R. 324 130.

1 Leave the car park by the exit road, cross the River Beane bridge into Port Hill B158. Turn L (S) downhill and at the tee junction at the foot of the hill, turn R into Port Vale. Follow this road (NW) past Mill Mead School L, to the end of the housing. Continue ahead (N) along the pleasant track through woodland which follows the river L to the old Molewood Pumping Station. Continue (NW) along the bank of the river R, go under a railway bridge to the main Hertford to Stevenage road A119 at a gate. Cross the A119, turn R and in a few metres turn L along a path through woodland (N) with the river L.

2 This path ends at the tarmac drive leading to the Georgian mansion of Goldings. Turn R along this drive to the A119, cross and turn L. In a few metres, take the path R which leads down to the river at Waterford Marshes. Follow this path (N) alongside the river L. Note the village of Waterford with its church spire L. Further on note the concrete storm conduit pipes numbered 276, 277 protruding from the ground. Continue by the river to the houses ahead, note the tennis court R, and emerge through a kissing gate into a road.

3 Turn R (E) along the road and in about 50m turn L into Barley Croft at the signpost. Go through the housing (N) to a stile by the last house number 21. Cross this and walk ahead (N) to another stile. Continue under the railway bridge to follow the river again. This path meets a tarmac road, turn L (NW) and in a few metres where the road turns L, bear R (N) passing a house L. Ignore the bend of this track, continue straight ahead (N) towards a wood. Go past a large barn L, and at a yellow waymark turn L down to the river. Follow this pleasant wooded path alongside the river L (N) to Stapleford Church.

4 Leave the churchyard by the gate, and turn L (W) along the road. Cross the bridge over the river and pass the village store L to meet the A119. Cross the road, turn R (N) and in a few metres turn L (NW) on a path alongside the village hall R. Continue under the railway bridge, and on emerging, turn R along a path (NW) by a power line post. Go diagonally across the field uphill through a hedge gap, then bear L (NW) downhill towards the farm in the distance. At the road bear L (W) along it.

5 Ignore the bridleway just before Great Gobions Farm, follow the waymarked path around the farm itself. Bear L (W) and follow the hedge R (SW) towards Bramfield Wood. Enter the wood through a hedge gap R. Bear L (S) along the permissive bridleway, ignore the stile R. Follow the red marker posts for about 1km. At the tee junction bear L (S) downhill to a road. Turn L (SE) along this road into the village of Bramfield. Here refreshments can be obtained at the Grandison Arms in the lane leading R from the village green.

6 Continue (S) out of the village on the road signed Tewin, go past the water works L. In about a further 1km, turn L (E) along a bridleway with hedge L. This eventually meets the Bramfield to Hertford road at a gate. Here turn R (SE) along this road with care. Continue past a shooting range R for about 1km to a turning L at the bottom of the hill.

7 Turn L (NE) along this private road at the signpost marked Broadoak End. Follow L and R through housing to a crossing track. Turn R (E) to enter the grassland in front of the Goldings mansion L. Walk diagonally across the meadow (NE) to a path leading to the main access road (E). At the driveway junction turn R (SE) signposted Hertford. Follow this driveway to the three bridges crossing the river Beane to item 2 above. Having crossed these bridges, turn R (S) to follow the path alongside the river R through woodland to the A119. Cross the road turn L to follow the river L to Port Vale, then L into Port Hill (Bengeo Road) and so back to the car park.

WALK 18

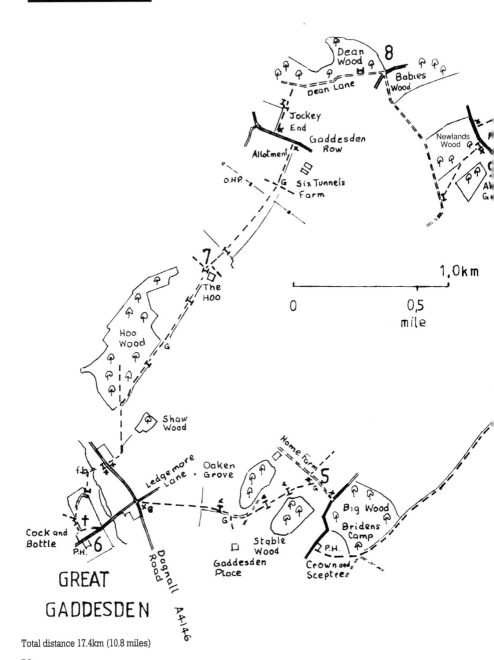

Total distance 17.4km (10.8 miles)

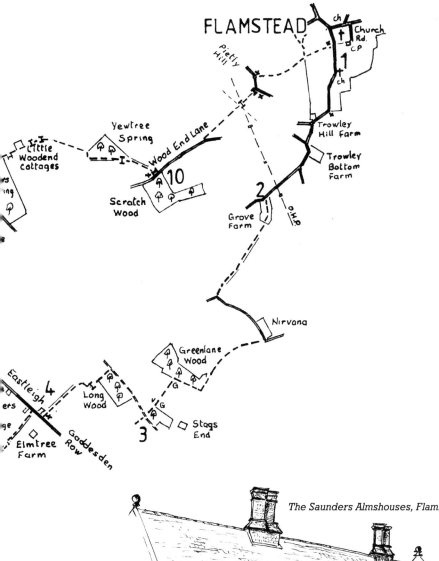

FLAMSTEAD

Pietly Hill

ch
Church Rd.
C P
1
ch

Yewtree Spring

Wood End Lane

Little Woodend cottages

10

Scratch Wood

Trowley Hill Farm

Trowley Bottom Farm

2

Grove Farm

O.H.P

Nirvana

Greenlane Wood

Eastleigh

Long Wood

G

VIG

3

Stags End

Elmtree Farm

Gaddesden Row

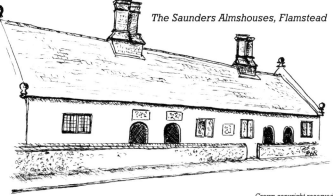

The Saunders Almshouses, Flamstead

Crown copyright reserved

57

FLAMSTEAD, GREAT GADDESDEN, JOCKEY END

WALK

18

Park in Flamstead Village Hall car park. G.R. 079 145.

1 Leave the car park (W) along the churchyard path, passing the church R into Trowley Hill Road where turn L (S) down this road. At Trowley Hill Farm R, turn L down White Hill (S). Pass Trowley Bottom Farm L, and take the R fork uphill (SW) to Grove Farm L. Enter the farmyard (S) and walk between buildings keeping to the gravel track which goes between a barn L and the main farm buildings R.

2 Continue (SW) up a well defined track with fence L to a transverse drovers way. Turn L (SE) along this grassy track to 'Nirvana' L. Where this track turns sharp L, turn R (SW) through a hedge gap into a field. Cross this to the SE corner of Greenlane Wood. Turn R (NW) along the edge of this wood R for 250m to an old gate R. Turn L (SW) across the field to the W side of the wood on the skyline, to an iron gate. Continue (SW) with wood L to a transverse bridleway.

3 Turn R (NW) along this with Longwood L. In 400m at the corner of the wood turn L (SW), with the edge of the wood L and wire fence R. Cross a stile turn R (NW) and in a few metres L (SW) with hedge R out to Gaddesden Row alongside 'Eastleigh'.

4 Turn R (NW) along this road and in 75m turn L (SW) into a path alongside Holly Cottage R. Continue (SW) with hedge L, and in 150m, at a hedge gap, go through and continue on a gravel track (SW) now with hedge R. This track leads to Bridens Camp R then bends (W) to the Crown and Sceptre P.H. Turn R (NE) along the road taking great care around the S bends. Turn L along Home Farm Lane.

5 After 75m cross the stile by a gate L into a field, continue (SW) over two more stiles heading for Great Gaddesden church. Cross a wide track and continue (W) with fence R to a waymarked gate. Go through and continue (W) now with fence L. Cross another stile, and across an open field to a signposted gate in Dagnall Road at its junction with Ledgemore Lane. Cross the road and enter Great Gaddesden village. Refreshments may be available at the Cock and Bottle P.H.

6 Walk up the short lane (W) through the lych gate into the churchyard. Pass the church R and cross a stile in the opposite corner. Turn sharp R (N) follow the churchyard wall to another stile R. Cross into a housing estate passing a row of garages L. At a sharp bend in the road continue N over a stile to the flood plain of the river Gade. Cross the footbridge (NE) to a stile on the A4146. Cross this road to a track beside a row of houses L. Follow the hedge R to a hedge corner, then take the path due N to a wooden barrier in Hoo Wood. Immediately on entering the wood, turn R (NE) to follow inside the wood boundary R. Cross a stile into a headland path (NE) now outside the wood boundary L. Go through a gate into a meadow with hedge R, cross a stile passing The Hoo house R.

7 Cross two more stiles (NE) into a wide meadow. Continue (NE) parallel to the hedge R but about 50m from it. After going under power lines, go through an iron gate into an allotment area L. This track leads to a signpost in Gaddesden Row. Turn L (NW) for 150m towards Jockey End to a row of houses R. Turn R (NE) at the signpost at the end of these houses, pass the small play area, and cross a stile into a headland path L. This leads down to a gap in the hedge in Dean Lane. Turn R (E) along this pleasant lane for about 700m to a road.

8 Cross the road to a track (S) into Babies Wood which may be muddy. Continue (SE) along the edge of Newlands Wood. In 75m beyond the far corner of the wood turn L over a stile into a field between Newlands Wood L and Abels Grove R. Continue to the signposted stile at the NE corner of the wood into a road.

9   Turn L and in 50m turn R (NE) along a lane to Little Woodend Cottages L. Continue (E) behind a shed, cross a stile (E) into a field, follow a hedge R to another stile into a field. Continue (ESE) to the right-hand corner of Yewtree Spring Wood. Here a path along the boundary of the wood goes (E) with wire fence L and hedge R. At the E corner of the wood, cross a stile and continue (ESE) along a field edge with fence L. Cross two more stiles into Wood End Lane.

10   Turn L (NE) and in 350m at a bend in the road, fork L (NE) into a field down to the bottom of the valley. Cross a stile immediately beneath the power lines and on (NE) up to another stile at Pietly Hill. Turn L along the road, and in 100m turn R into a field. Continue (NE) towards Flamstead Church, into the churchyard path, and so back to the car park.

Near Home Farm, Bridens Camp

WALK 19

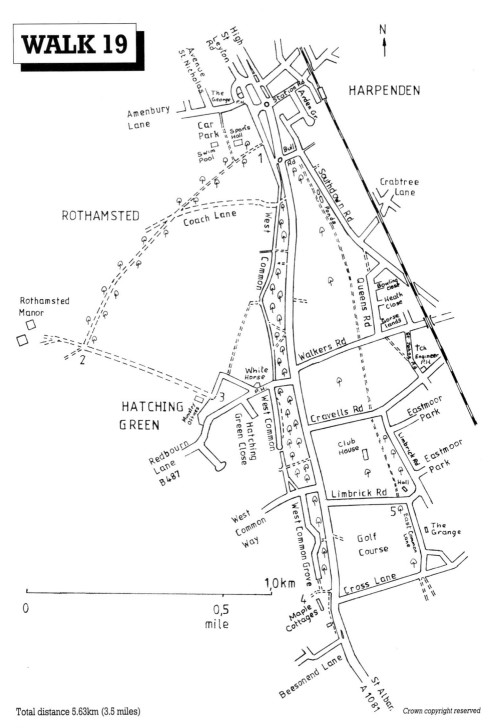

Total distance 5.63km (3.5 miles)

Crown copyright reserved

ROTHAMSTED PARK, HARPENDEN COMMON

A short walk suitable for families with push chairs.

WALK 19

By bus: Alight at the George P.H. at the south end of the High Street, Harpenden, bear R into Leyton Road, continue south to the entrance of Rothamsted Park.

By train: Turn L down Station Road to the High Street, then cross and bear L into Leyton Road to the entrance of Rothamsted Park.

By car: Park in Amenbury Lane car park, go south into Rothamsted Park past the Sports Hall L. Turn R along the avenue of trees.

1 Enter Rothamsted Park by the brick gate posts marked 'James Marshall House' opposite the town sign on the green. Continue (SW) through the avenue of lime trees ignoring the fork in the track.

2 At the tee junction with another avenue note the out buildings of Rothamsted Manor R. Turn L (SE) along this avenue to the entrance at the offices of the Ministry of Agriculture, Fisheries and Food R, where emerge on to Hatching Green.

3 Continue L then R round the green, passing the White Horse public house L into Redbourn Lane. Turn L and in a few metres R (S) into West Common which in places becomes a path. At West Common Way turn L and almost at once R (S) into West Common Grove. Keep to the L side of this road noting a pleasant path just inside the tree line.

4 At the end of the carriage way, a path continues (S) through the trees to a transverse path at Maple Cottages. Turn L (E) to the main St Albans road A1081. Turn R (S) along this to a bollard island where it is safe to cross this busy road. Retrace your steps (N) on the other side, then turn R (E) into Cross Lane. Continue (E) to a cross roads where turn L (N) along East Common Lane.

5 At the tee junction opposite Limbrick Hall, turn L and in a few metres R (N) on a path along the edge of the golf course, parallel with the bridle path (N). Cross Cravells Road (N) then Walkers Road (N). At two crossing tracks, keep R to a cinder track with ponds R. Keep parallel with the line of ponds to Bull Road back to the starting point L.

Alternatively in wet weather at item 5 facing Limbrick Hall, turn R and then L along Limbrick Road. At the junction with Cravells Road turn R (E) by the post box. At the 'Engineer' public house, turn L (N) into St Johns Road, then opposite the vicarage, fork L on to a path to Walkers Road. Cross into Queens Road, and where this turns R, keep ahead (N) on a path to Southdown Road. Continue (N) using the pavement on the opposite side passing three ponds L. Turn L into Bull Road back to the starting point.

Hatching Green

61

WALK 20

Pond at Hammonds End Farm

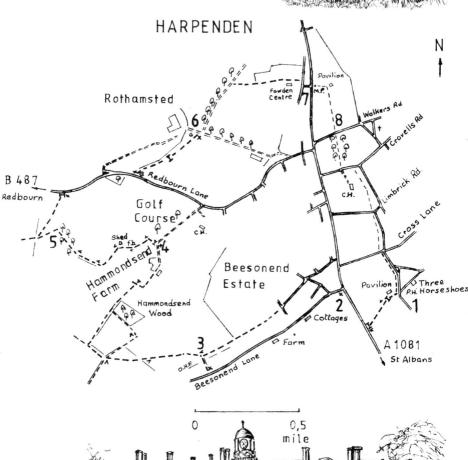

HARPENDEN

Total distance 10.0km (6.2 miles)   *Rothamsted Manor*   Crown copyright reserved

HAMMONDSEND, ROTHAMSTED, HARPENDEN COMMON

Park on Harpenden Common, in car park near the Three Horseshoes public house.
G.R. 144 120

1 From the car park, cross East Common Lane (SW) and the golf course, passing Bamville Wood Cricket Pavilion R. Cross the stile behind the pavilion and the field (SW) heading for the L of the White House, formerly called the Horse and Jockey. Cross the stile into St Albans Road A1081, cross this road and turn R (N).

2 In 300m at the Harpenden Town sign, turn L (W) along Beesonend Lane. Continue past the modern Beesonend Estate R, and the Childwick estate cottages and farm L. After almost 1.2km, turn R (N) at the footpath sign, continue with hedge R. Pass under power lines to the end of the hedge and a waymark post, where turn L (W).

3 Continue (W) along a clear path through crops towards a distant white house. Go through a hedge gap down to a transverse track by a large tree. Continue ahead (NW) with hedge R. In 150m look for a path R (NW) entered by climbing the field edge bank. Continue (NE) with hedge R. Ignore a track from R, but continue (NE) along the boundary of Hammondsend Wood R and the golf course R. At the next transverse track turn R and follow as it bends L, passing barns R and Hammondsend Farm and House L.

4 At the bend in the access road continue ahead (NW), cross the signposted stile into a paddock with hedge L. Cross another stile, bear L into the golf course. Follow the boundary fence L (W), cross the ditch at the plank bridge, continue through a woodland strip along the edge of the course. Pass a wooden shed R, turn L (SW) following the edge of the course to number 8 tee. Here turn R (NW) into a woodland strip along the course boundary L.

5 On emerging into a field by a power line post, turn R and almost immediately L (SW) along a hedge L. At the next gap in a transverse hedge by a power pole, do not go through, but turn sharp R (NNE) across a field. Head for the R end of the bar fence where it joins a hedge. Cross the signposted stile down a steep bank into Redbourn Lane. Turn R along the verge of this busy road, passing Redbourn Lodge L. In 600m turn L (NE) through an iron gate into a meadow. Cross a stile and continue with wire fence L passing the delightful Rothamsted Manor L.

6 Go through the signposted iron gate, cross the drive into a tree line drive ahead (NNE). In 450m bear R (E) along a macadam road ignoring the gravel path ahead. This is the service road to Rothamsted Experimental Station and is a public footpath. Go past the laboratories and the new Fowden Conference Hall R.

7 Leave Rothamsted passing the Administration building L, cross two transverse roads (E) on to Harpenden Common, noting the old milestone 'London 25 miles'. Bear R past the cricket pavilion L. bear R again (S). Follow a track along the centre of the Common to Walkers Road, ignore the track L towards the housing.

8 Cross this road (S) into the tree gap opposite. Continue through the trees to Cravells Road. Turn L (E) and just before the entrance to Eastmoor Park, follow the bridleway R (S) by the horseshoe waymark. Keep to this bridleway along the L edge of the golf course, and look out for flying golf balls. Cross two roads and at Bamville Wood cricket pitch, bear L to the 'Three Horseshoes' and the car park.

Flowton Priory, Harpenden

WALK 21

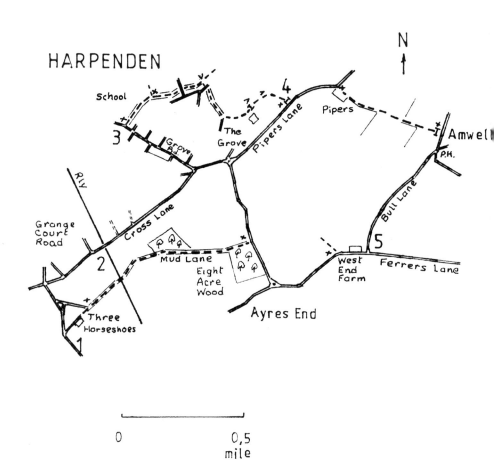

HARPENDEN

School

3

The Grove

Grove Rd

Pipers Lane

Pipers

4

Amwell

P.H.

Rly

Cross Lane

Bull Lane

Grange Court Road

2

Mud Lane

Eight Acre Wood

West End Farm

5

Ferrers Lane

Three Horseshoes

Ayres End

N

0   0,5
           mile

Total distance 8.0km (5.0 miles)
Figure of eight walks 20 and 21, 18km (10.3 miles)

Crown copyright reserved

HARPENDEN, THE GROVE, AMWELL

Park on Harpenden Common car park near the Three Horseshoes P.H. G.R. 144 120.

1 From the 'Three Horseshoes' car park, turn R (NE). Keep forward past the bridleway sign, turn L (NW) in front of 'The Cottage'. Continue forward (N) then fork R on to East Common to a post box on a pole. Turn R (E) at the cross roads into Cross Lane.

2 Continue over railway bridge with housing L and Cross Farm R, to Grove Road where turn L (NW). In 500m alongside number 50 Grove Road, turn R (NE) along a signed bridleway.

3 Continue (NE) with housing R and a school L. Keep forward at the path fork, cross a minor road, and continue forward. Look for a waymark and take the fenced path R (S) between gardens. Cross another road and continue forward to the buildings at Grove Farm. Bear L and cross the stile ahead at a waymarked gate. Continue past a yellow cottage L along a grassy track to a stile by a gate into Pipers Lane.

4 Turn L (NE) and in 300m take the path R (E) alongside Pipers Farm. Continue with hedge R, cross a field to a hedge gap by a single tree. Go forward over a stile into Down Green Lane where turn R into Amwell. Bear R (SW) along the lane past the 'Elephant and Castle'. Turn R into Bull Lane.

5 At the next tee junction, turn R (W) along Ferrers Lane past West End Farm. Ignore the path R, and continue to the grass triangle at the road junction. Turn R (N) into Ayres End Lane. Pass Eight Acre Wood L and at the boundary of the wood turn L (W) into the aptly named bridleway 'Mud Lane'. Notice the regenerated pond just inside the wood near its W end which is part of the conservation activity by the Dickenson brothers of Cross Farm. The bridleway continues over the railway back to the 'Three Horseshoes' car park.

Note: Walks 20 and 21 can be combined, making a figure of eight all day walk.

West End Farm, Nomansland

65

WALK 22

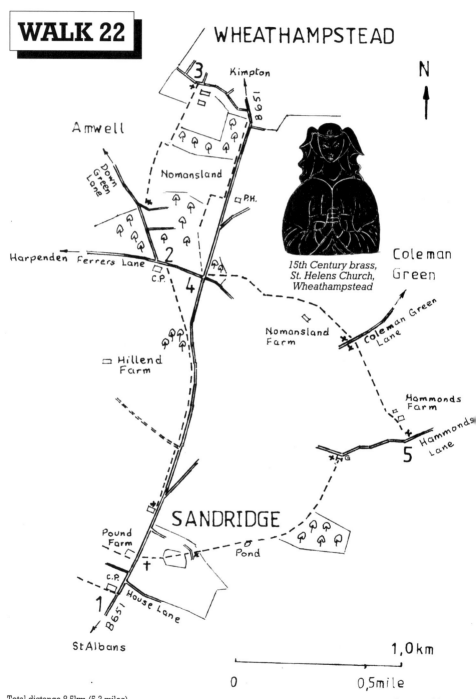

WHEATHAMPSTEAD

Kimpton

B651

N

Amwell

Down Green Lane

Nomansland

P.H.

15th Century brass,
St. Helens Church,
Wheathampstead

Harpenden   Ferrers Lane

C.P.

Coleman Green

Coleman Green Lane

Nomansland Farm

Hillend Farm

Hammonds Farm

Hammonds Lane

SANDRIDGE

Pound Farm

Pond

C.P.

House Lane

B651

St Albans

1,0 km

0   0,5mile

Total distance 8.5km (5.3 miles)

Crown copyright reserved

SANDRIDGE, WHEATHAMPSTEAD

Park in the public car park in Sandridge by the Village Hall. G.R. 169 104.

1 From the car park, turn L (N) along the St Albans Road B651. Continue through the village to the former school L now offices. Here at the signpost bear L and continue (N) parallel to the road along a field edge with hedge R for 1.5km. Where this path turns R to the road, go through the hedge, bear diagonally L (NW) across Nomansland Common towards the car park on the Common.

2 Cross Ferrers Lane and go up Down Green Lane opposite (N) for 300m. At the second road junction turn R and in 10m L (N) at the signpost. In 15m cross a stile and continue (N) past a farmyard R and a young planted copse of Christmas trees then of mature trees. Follow the path R then L round the bottom edge of a field following the boundary of a wood R. In 20m from this corner, bear R into the wood, bear L (N) through the wood along a fenced path past a former school R.

3 At the road turn R (E) and continue to the junction with St Albans Road B651. At the signpost turn R (S) along a downhill path with road and hedge L to the bottom corner of field edge. Here turn R (W) following the fence L. At the corner turn L, and continue (S) out to the cricket ground.

4 Bear L (S) round the field towards the cross roads. Here turn L (E) and follow the bridle path sign. Continue (E) along this path bearing slightly R. At the hedge bear L and continue (SE) with hedge R to Coleman Green Lane. Cross and continue (SE) with hedge R through Hammonds Farm into a track between brick gate posts out to Hammonds Lane.

5 Turn R (W) along the lane and in 400m at the signpost turn L over a stile. Follow the path (SW) with hedge R into a wood. On emerging from this continue (SW) with hedge L towards Sandridge passing a small pond L. This path continues between fields across Langley Grove. Continue passing allotments R, to the church L and into the St Albans Road. Turn L back to the car park.

Amwell

67

WALK 23

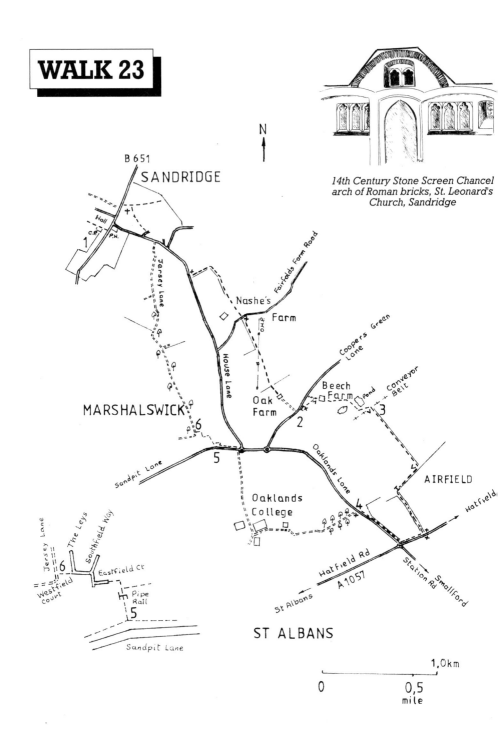

14th Century Stone Screen Chancel arch of Roman bricks, St. Leonard's Church, Sandridge

Total distance 10.0km (6.2 miles)

Crown copyright reserved

SANDRIDGE, OAKLANDS, JERSEY LANE

Park in the public car park in Sandridge by the Village Hall. G.R. 169 104.

1 From the car park turn L (N) along the B651. In 100m turn R (SE) along House Lane for 1km. Turn L (NE) at the signposted track which goes uphill with hedge R. In 200m the path turns R (SE). Go past Nashes Farm R and cross Fairfolds Farm road. Continue (SE) with wire fence R then through a hedge gap to Oak Farm. Keep on the farm access road to Coopers Green Lane.

2 Turn L (NE) and in 60m turn R at the stile and signpost, into a small wood. Continue (NE) into an access road where turn R to Beech Farm. Follow the waymarks through the farm (E) along a gravel road between ponds. This bends L then turns R (SE) at a small bridge over a conveyor belt.

3 A well marked track continues (SE) with hedge L towards a large iron gate at the airfield boundary. Here turn R (SW) in front of the gate, and with hedge L continue to a stile. Cross and turn L (SE) following the airfield boundary L between chain link fences to meet the Hatfield Road. Turn R (SE) along the road passing Notcutts Garden Centre R. At the roundabout turn R (NW) along Oaklands Lane. A path runs between the housing and the hedge bordering the road. In about 400m, cross the road into the signposted access road to Oaklands College.

4 This tree lined asphalt road continues (W) towards the main farm buildings. At the tee junction turn R (N) along a wide gravel track between farm buildings which emerges on to Sandpit Lane. Cross and turn L (W) along the boundary of Jersey Farm housing estate.

5 After about 250m just before the path bends L, turn R (N) along a path by a house with a conservatory. Go through a pipe rail barrier, and immediately turn L (W) into Eastfield Court. At the road junction tee, turn R and in a few metres turn L (W) into Westfield Court. Where this bends R, continue ahead in front of housing into Jersey Lane.

6 Turn R (N) along this tree lined lane and in about 2km this emerges on to House Lane. Here turn L (NW) along this lane to Sandridge Village. Turn L (SW) along the B651 to the car park.

NOTE : There are a number of public houses in Sandridge where refreshment is available.

This walk can be linked with number 22 to form a figure of eight all day walk.

Sandridge

WALK 24

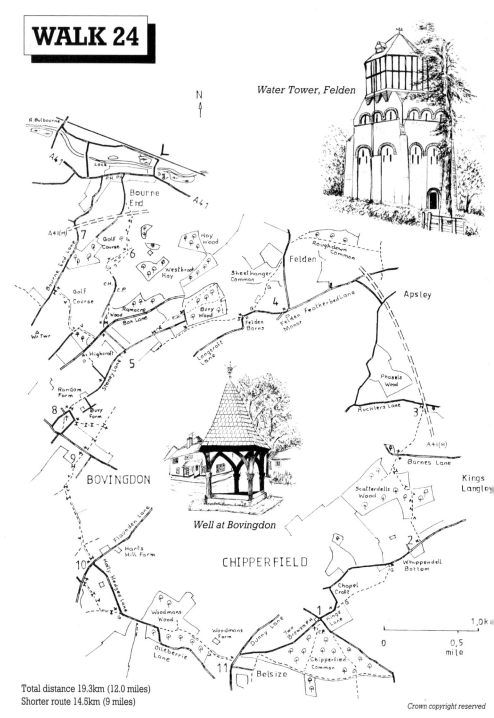

Water Tower, Felden

Well at Bovingdon

Total distance 19.3km (12.0 miles)
Shorter route 14.5km (9 miles)

Crown copyright reserved

70

CHIPPERFIELD, FELDEN, BOURNE END, BOVINGDON

Park in public car park alongside St Pauls Church, Chipperfield. G.R. 044 016.

1 Walk past the Two Brewers P.H. (NE) and cross the road into Kings Lane. Where the road turns L, continue ahead (NE) along a gravel path, then cross an open field. After a short R and L, go through an old waymarked stile gap, and bear L (NE) across another field. This path emerges through a gate on to the road. Turn R (NE) down to Whippendell Bottom.

2 At the rise of the road, opposite Kings Langley Riding School, turn L (NW) on to a concrete path alongside a large house. Keep forward between meadows. At the tree line turn R then L, and follow the waymarks on trees in the woodland. At the wood boundary, cross a stile and bear R (NE) across a field. Cross Barnes Lane and continue (NE) heading for the L end of a wood ahead.

3 At the A41 (M) motorway turn L then shortly R over a stile into Rucklers Lane. Turn L (W) along this lane for 800m passing Phasels Wood, the Herts County Scout Camping Ground R. Where the lane bends L, turn R (N) into a bridleway by the boundary fence of this Camp R. In about 1km on reaching the road turn L (NW), do not cross the motorway bridge. Go downhill, bear L (W) into Featherbed Lane. In 800m at a four way junction keep ahead (W).

4 In a further 100m opposite Felden Manor, turn R at a signpost 'Longcroft 1/4'. In 400m just past Felden Barns, where the lane turns L, bear R (W) over a stile on to a clear path across fields. Continue forward to meet Bury Wood R. At the end of the wood turn R (N) into it, at a wooden signpost. In about 100m, at a transverse path turn L then R into a road (N). In a further 30m at a signpost, turn L (W) on a path between housing fences. Bear L across a field to a signpost, cross a stile into Stoney Lane, turn R.

5 Take the next turning R (NW) opposite 'Huntsmoor'. At Box Lane turn R, cross the road with care, and in 20m turn L on to a tarmac driveway. Bear R (N) opposite Little Hay Cottage, cross a stile into woodland. On reaching the golf course, follow the path signs up the access road. Pass the car park R, and the club house L, follow the road bend L past the large buildings R. Follow the waymarks (NE) past the bungalow R.

6 At a signpost turn L (N) across the golf course past a small copse L. Follow the footpath signs downhill (N) towards a tall tree. Here bear L and cross the motorway, (a footbridge is currently being built). Continue ahead (N) cross a field, then a stile, go along a grassy track to the A41 opposite the Village Hall in Bourne End. Here turn L (W) where refreshments may be obtained at the White Horse P.H., the Anchor P.H. or the Little Chef.

7 Here turn L (S) into Bourne End Lane. Go under the motorway and continue uphill (SW) until the road levels. Turn L (SE) along a bridleway alongside the golf course L. Follow waymarks out to the main entrance to the golf course in Box Lane. Cross, turn R (SW) and in 250m turn L on a path signed 'Bovingdon' between gate posts, just before the Highcroft entrance. Follow this through a R and L to Stoney Lane where turn R (SW).

8 At a road, turn L (SE) alongside Bovingdon churchyard R. In 100m where the road turns R, keep ahead (SE) across a stile. Cross two more stiles (E) to another by a four way signpost at the field corner. Do not cross this stile, but turn sharp R (SW) with hedge L. Continue through housing to the Bovingdon/Chipperfield road. Cross, turn R, and in 20m turn L (SW) at a sign into housing.

9 Continue (SW) along the pavement then ahead between numbers 51 and 52. Cross a stile (SW) into a field with hedge R. cross another stile, bear L to the opposite field corner. At the next stile, cross and bear L (S) on a path marked BV14. Cross the field to a stile at the L end of a hedge. Continue (S) with hedge L then hedge R to a stile. Ignore this, bear L (SE) along BV14 with fence R out to Flaunden Lane.

10 Turn R (SW) and in 300m opposite Water Lane turn L (SE), cross a stile into a path with hedge R. Cross another stile, continue to a R corner of a field, go through a gap, and turn immediately L (E) with hedge L. Cross a field, continue (E) into Holly Hedges Lane, where turn R (SE). Go past 'no horses' sign L, and where the lane turns R, bear L (E) through a gap in a wooden barrier signed 'Belsize 3/4' into Woodmans Wood. This clear path passes a pole barrier R, then goes uphill (E) with wire fence R. On emerging from the wood, continue ahead (E) with hedge L. down to Dunny Lane. Here cross and turn R (SW).

11 In 100m turn L go up Little Windmill Hill. At the last bungalow turn L (N) to join a woodland track (NE) which leads to another bearing R (E). Continue (E) through woodland with houses R. Immediately before a gated barrier turn L (NE) along a wide path signed 'no horse riding'. A short R and L emerges on to the cricket pitch on Chipperfield Common. Go behind the pavilion (N) alongside the church wall L to the car park.

Note: This walk may be shortened at item 5 by continuing along Stoney Lane (SW) to Bovingdon Church. Then continue from item 8 to 11.

BIBLIOGRAPHY

HERTFORDSHIRE WALKS BOOKLETS

1. Afoot in Hertfordshire, D. Veall, Spurbooks Ltd., 1979.
2. Discovering Walks in Hertfordshire, Ron Pigram, Shire Publications, 1985
3. Footpath Walks in Mid Herts. for Motorists, vols 1, 2, 3, Mid Herts. Footpaths Soc., 1986.
4. Hertfordshire Chain Walk, East Herts. Footpaths Society, Castlemead Publications, 1987.
5. Hertfordshire Rambles, Liz Moynihan, Countryside Books, 1988.
6. Local Walks, South Beds, North Chilterns, Vaughan Basham, Book Castle, 1988.
7. Walk Herts and Bucks, David Perrott, Laurence Main, Bartholomew, 1990.
8. Walks for Motorists, Chilterns Northern Area, Nicholas Moon, Frederick Warne, 1982.
9. Walks in Dacorum, Dacorum Borough Council, 1986.
10. Walks in Hertfordshire, Frank Dawes, Spurbooks Ltd., 1975.
11. Walks in the Hertfordshire Chilterns, Nicholas Moon, Shire Publications, 1986.

WALKS LEAFLETS

12. Upper Lea Valley Through Walk, Upper Lea Valley Liaison Group, Herts. County Council.
13. Ver/Colne Valley Walk, County Planning Department, Herts. County Council.

Admin Press Ltd., Gazelda Industrial Estate, Lower High Street, Watford, Herts. WD1 2JL